When Everybody Ate at

SCHRAFFT'S

Other Books By
Joan Kanel Slomanson

A Short History:
Thumbnail Sketches of 50 Little Giants

Baby's First Book of Trauma

How To Stop Smoking For $1

Co-author of *Fanny Hillman on Campus*

Co-author of *Fanny Hillman in Washington*

Joan Kanel Slomanson

When Everybody Ate at
SCHRAFFT'S

MEMORIES, PICTURES,
AND RECIPES FROM A
VERY SPECIAL
RESTAURANT EMPIRE

BARRICADE BOOKS
FORT LEE, NEW JERSEY

Published by Barricade Books Inc.
185 Bridge Plaza North
Suite 308-A
Fort Lee, NJ 07024

www.barricadebooks.com

A copy of the Library of Congress Cataloging-in-Publication Data
may be obtained upon request from the Library of Congress.

ISBN 1-56980-335-8
ISBN-13 978-1-56980-335-6

First Printing

Book Design by Pauline Neuwirth, Neuwirth & Associates, Inc.

Manufactured in the United States of America

To my friend, Frank Shattuck, great-grandson
and namesake of the founding father of Schrafft's
—and to the other members of the Shattuck family

It gives me great pleasure

to see this book about Schrafft's in print.

Thanks, Joan, for telling the whole story so well!

Frank Shattuck

Contents

Acknowledgments

AS YOU WILL SEE throughout the book, I have many people to thank for contributing their recollections of Schrafft's. Moreover, I am deeply indebted to three wonderful men: Frank Shattuck for suggesting the book and lending me the voluminous recipe files; Allan Wilson for bringing my manuscript to the attention of Barricade Books and encouraging me; and Woody Slomanson for fine-tuning all the illustrations and helping me in countless other ways. Barricade VP Jeff Nordstedt was very helpful. In addition, a big vote of thanks goes to Carole Stuart for her continuous support and editorial guidance.

PERMISSIONS GRATEFULLY RECEIVED:

Eileen Markey for permission to reprint Schrafft's menus and other mementos from the Raymond J. Markey Family Collection.

"A Pox on You My Goodly Host" by S.J. Perelman reprinted by permission of Harold Ober Associates Incorporated. First published in *The New Yorker*. Copyright © 1941 by S.J. Perelman. Copyright renewed © 1968 by S.J. Perelman.

Judith Jones for permission to use the recipes she adapted for Schrafft's Butterscotch Cookies and Chewy Oatmeal Cookies, and also the Cheese Bread recipe from *Knead It, Punch It, Bake It,* copyright © 1998, 1981 by Judith and Evan Jones. By permission of Houghton Mifflin Company.

Special Collections, Eric V. Hauser Memorial Library, Reed College for permission to reprint the recipe "Stuffed Breast of Chicken with Mushroom Sauce" from *Beard on Birds,* copyright © 1989, 2001, by Reed College.

The Cartoon Bank, a division of *The New Yorker,* for permission to reprint the Helen Hokinson cartoon captioned "Sometimes I think Schrafft's doesn't *care* about calories."

From the Library of Congress, Prints and Photographs Division, Gottscho–Schleisner Collection. Images in this collection have been placed in the public domain by the heirs of the photographers.

The Orange-Apricot-Pecan Coffee Cake recipe. From *The Good Enough to Eat Breakfast Cookbook* by Carrie Levin. Copyright © 2001 by Carrie Levin. By permission of Warner Books, Inc.

Michael Cumella for permission to reprint cover of Schrafft's Play-A-Tune.

(The Rev.) Joan B. Horwitt for permission to reprint the words of the song "Schrafft's" by Arnold B. Horwitt.

Two Gottscho-Schleisner photographs of the Schrafft's at 61 Fifth Avenue, from the Museum of the City of New York.

When Everybody Ate at

SCHRAFFT'S

Foreword

GEORGE LANG

WHEN I READ the manuscript about Schrafft's, it reminded me of my first years in this wonderful country and the great city of New York.

I arrived in New York City in 1946, and I had to use everything I had plus the luck that came with it in order to survive. I passed by Schrafft's many times, and the very first meal I was able to afford there was a wonderful breakfast, which of course Schrafft's was justly famous for. These days, when most restaurants succeed by serving vintage mineral water, by reading *When Everybody Ate at Schrafft's* you can escape from the cement shoes of today's culinary styles. Frank G. Shattuck, the founder of Schrafft's, defined their food as "American home cooking," and the countless Schrafft's restaurants served their guests the kinds of dishes many of us around the restaurant-world are trying to create, serve, and enjoy.

George Lang's Cafe des Artistes has flourished for many decades—just as Schrafft's once did.

ONCE UPON A time there were famous restaurants named Schrafft's—more than fifty of them in New York City and other parts of the Northeast, plus a bevy of beautiful restaurant/motor inns from New England to Florida. Memories of Schrafft's came flooding back to me when Frank Shattuck, a great-grandson of the founding father, Frank G. Shattuck, asked me to write a book about the restaurants. What I remember most was surrendering to coffee ice cream smothered in hot butterscotch sauce and sprinkled with almonds. Priced at well under a dollar, it was all that I could afford on the salary of my first job out of college.

HOT BUTTERSCOTCH SAUCE, SCHRAFFT'S STYLE

1 stick butter
½ cup heavy cream
1 cup brown sugar
1 tsp. vanilla extract
½ cup light corn syrup

1. In medium saucepan, combine butter, sugar and corn syrup.
2. Cook, stirring, just until mixture is thick and smooth.
3. Turn off heat, stir in heavy cream and vanilla. Serve on ice cream, of course, with nuts on top of it all.

In one way or another, it seems as if just about everybody who visited Schrafft's "stores," as the management called them, recalls the experience. Of course, if you remember eating there, by now you're probably a little "long in the tooth." Never mind! Let's look back . . .

- ❧ Waitresses, uniformly dressed in black with crisp, white collars and cuffs and dainty, white aprons, were often Irishwomen right off the boat. (A friend of mine, Jerry Falk, jokingly insists that they were all named Bridget.)
- ❧ The virtue of eating simple Schrafft's dishes was lost when one gave in, as most customers inevitably did, to the outrageously calorific desserts. The rotund women in Helen Hokinson's *New Yorker* cartoons vouch for this.
- ❧ Schrafft's was one of a rare breed of restaurants where a woman could dine alone while discreetly sipping alcoholic beverages. The drink list was

long and colorful, ranging from Manhattans and Martinis to Grasshoppers, Golden Fizzes, and Pink Ladies.

- ❧ Not just for the ladies, well-dressed business-men were often seen at Schrafft's, slurping down bluepoint oysters with their cocktails. (And then there is the story about a Brooklyn girl trying to affect a fancy accent in Schrafft's by ordering "ersters on the hahf shell.")

- ❧ Large family groups gathered to gobble up cheeseburgers, sundaes and full-course meals. In and out of New York, going to Schrafft's with one's children was often a special-occasion treat.

- ❧ A favorite haunt of theatre-goers, Schrafft's also had its share of employees who became success-ful actors. John Forsythe, Kirk Douglas, and John Dall waited tables while waiting for stardom, and Robert Morse worked at one of the retail counters.

- ❧ Along with baked goods and ice cream to take home, Schrafft's own candy was always promi-nently displayed in the windows and front part of the stores, Chocolates were, after all, how the business got its start.

Restaurants come and go—and mostly go—but the Schrafft's culinary and confectionary empire grew and flourished decade after decade, setting the stage for many of today's restaurant chains, but with a polish and personality all its own. Then, in the late 1970s this outpost of middle-class civility began to fade out of the picture and it was a mere shadow of its former self after that.

With the passing of the Schrafft's era, I picture the wind blowing through those once lively, now deserted stores as if they were buildings in a western ghost town. Of course, the spaces may now be filled with dumpy fast-food emporiums or in tonier neighborhoods, savings banks, cellphone stores, and even bookshops. But in my mind's eye, Schrafft's lives on there.

IF SOME (BUT certainly not all) of the recipes included in this book seem a bit dated, well of course they are. Times change. Tastes change. But nostalgia or historical interest can whet one's appetite for Schrafft's dishes all over again.

How many ways will you enjoy SCHRAFFT'S today?

SCHRAFFT'S ICE CREAM
Almost 50 delicious flavors. In half-pints, pints, quarts, half-gallons. Ices, too. And ice milks and fresh fruit sherbets. At Schrafft's, and selected food outlets in Metropolitan New York.

SCHRAFFT'S RESTAURANTS
At more than 30 restaurants in Metropolitan New York, 12 million patrons a year enjoy quality food and individual attention.

SCHRAFFT'S CATERING SERVICE
At home or office, for a few friends or a crowd, large budget or small — Schrafft's helps you select just the right menu for the occasion . . . and then does everything for you.

SCHRAFFT'S FROZEN FOODS
Now you can serve Schrafft's most popular dishes in your home! Buy them at supermarkets and grocers in Metropolitan N.Y. area and New England. Also, at your local Schrafft's retail store or restaurant.

SCHRAFFT'S BAKED GOODS
If you think Schrafft's award-winning Apple Pie is good, try the breads, cakes, and pies on sale at our retail counters! Such a wide variety that choosing is almost as much fun as eating them.

SCHRAFFT'S FOOD SERVICE FOR BUSINESS
At more than 100 companies, coast-to-coast, Schrafft's designs and operates dining rooms for as few as ten persons, or cafeterias serving thousands. And, at more than 1,000 companies, Schrafft's serves a total of 30 million cups of coffee annually from its coffee wagons.

SCHRAFFT'S RESTAURANTS/MOTOR INNS
From New England to Florida, Schrafft's greets you on the road with luxurious, air-conditioned rooms. TV, of course. Swimming pools. Lavish cocktail lounges. And Schrafft's famous food.

SCHRAFFT'S CANDY
An astonishing variety — from peppermint sticks to sumptuous Gold Chest assortments — available at thousands of U.S. outlets, plus Schrafft's restaurants and retail outlets. Always fresh, attractively packaged, surpassingly delicious!

Here's a fact-packed page rescued out of Schrafft's past . . .

From Candy Salesman to Culinary King in One Fell Swoop

IT IS DIFFICULT to picture New York and the Northeast through the first seven decades of the twentieth century without seeing the urban landscape dotted with the restaurants that Schrafft's called "stores." It is also hard to imagine that a young candy drummer peddling his wares in parts of New England could swiftly build such an empire and transform himself into such a classy entrepreneur, becoming a millionaire at forty-five.

According to a profile of him in a 1928 issue of *The New Yorker,* Frank Garrett Shattuck was "an up-country boy" who at age twenty-three took the train to Poughkeepsie to sell candy to support his young wife and a small baby. In his itinerant life, Shattuck stopped off in Boston.

There, he met up with a Viennese confectioner, William F. Schraft, who at some point added an extra "f" to his name, giving birth to the name of the chain that would come into being. Boston was then the nation's candy capital and W.F. Schrafft's boxed chocolates were a star attraction. Frank G. Shattuck was so impressed with the product, he talked Schrafft into letting him try to boost sales on commission outside of New England. To promote the candy, Shattuck opened a small retail establishment using the Schrafft name. His first New York City store, opened on Broadway in 1898, took up a smidgen of space where Macy's huge department store now stands.

The early confectionery and soda fountain stores came out of an idea of Shattuck's sister, Jane, who helped to grow the business by suggesting that ice cream and later, lunches be served. As explained in *Fast Food* by John A. Jakie and Keith A. Sculle, restaurant customers as well as the cooks and the counter and table help in the United States were originally men. As women joined the restaurant work force and the working world in general, female customers came on the scene. No restaurateur spotted this trend sooner or exploited it better than the V.I.P.s at Schrafft's. In particular, Frank G. Shattuck targeted "secretaries and stenographers who must watch their pocketbooks."

By 1915, in addition to the store in Boston, there were nine in Manhattan, one in Brooklyn, and one in Syracuse. By 1934, there were 42. *The WPA Guide To New York City,* which was *The Federal Writers' Project Guide To 1930s New*

WHEN EVERYBODY ATE AT SCHRAFFT'S

Decisions,
decisions!
A customer
ponders over
which box of
chocolates to buy.

From father to son—the practice of lining up the waitresses for a regular morning inspection.

WHEN EVERYBODY ATE AT SCHRAFFT'S

York, said there were 38 branches of Schrafft's in the metropolitan area alone. They are listed among American restaurants in the Financial District, Greenwich Village, 34th St. District, Times Square, and Midtown East Side with "liquor served at most branches."

By 1950, there were more than 50 Schrafft's locations throughout New York's five boroughs plus a sprinkling of stores in Boston; Philadelphia; Syracuse; Newark, New Jersey; and in White Plains and New Rochelle, New York. All sold the ubiquitous boxed chocolates and packaged ice cream while serving breakfasts, lunches, dinners, and suppers.

"100% quality without the fancy foreign names"

That's a typical quote from Frank G. Shattuck who also described his food as "Plain, clean, wholesome American cooking." In a day and age when restaurants were either greasy spoons or pompous, pricey establishments with menus printed in French, Frank G. was determined to serve unpretentious, but tasty food at reasonable prices. Despite the complex recipes that originally made her famous, Julia Child once said, "You don't have to cook fancy or complicated masterpieces—just good food from fresh ingredients." Sounds like words right out of Frank G.'s mouth! Needless to say, he included none of the dishes we call ethnic—except for a tasty westernized curry—instead featuring what he considered good old home-style fare. To this end, he drove a hard bargain with suppliers to get the best possible ingredients and he ran a tight ship.

Fastidious about everything Schrafft's served and how it was served, Frank G. insisted that his waitresses go through an inspection for neatness and cleanliness every time they reported for work—a practice continued by Gerald Shattuck when he succeeded his father as company president. Like a sleuth hunting for damaging clues, Frank G. would go from one store to another to ferret out chipped tableware or poorly cleaned counters and fixtures.

Moreover, according to that 1928 *New Yorker* profile, this hard taskmaster would try out each new dish he came across on the menu, ask the waitresses innocent-sounding questions about it, and send it back to the kitchen if it didn't come up to his standards. He was even known to hurl a dishful of food that he considered to be of inferior quality into the middle of the offending restaurant.

Coffee also was under inspection and subject to rigid rules. Largely in an era when espresso was only served in Italian eateries, every cup of Schrafft's java had the distinction of tasting as if it too was brewed to order. Thirty minutes was the longest length of time any batch of coffee was allowed to exist and it has been said that some staffers could actually tell the age by the smell.

A ROUND-THE-CLOCK WORKAHOLIC

THIS INCREDIBLY DEDICATED restaurateur often lived like a simple merchant, "over the store." He had a luxury suite

The four Shattuck brothers, Frank, Harold, John, Gerald, taste-testing chocolate sodas. The managers were also expected to be expert tasters.

sweeping across an entire floor in New York's posh, new Hotel Pierre (where on his death in 1937 his glass-covered coffin was displayed). Yet throughout his years as president of Schrafft's, he maintained apartments above the stores because he often worked so late and woke up so early, he liked to sleep as near as possible to the job.

Although Frank G. had to be a hard act to follow, his four sons, Frank M., Harold, John, and Gerald, proved it could be done. As the crown princes of their father's kingdom, they bought only the best ingredients yet managed to keep prices reasonable. They taste-tested different dishes while insisting that the store managers sample every new batch of food. On top of it all, these second-generation Shattuck executives learned early on from their father to do well financially not only for the stores, but also for themselves. In a letter to his sons, which follows, he as much as told them to be personal penny pinchers.

LETTERS FROM FRANK G. AND FRANK M.

HERE'S THE ADVICE, built around his own work ethic, that Frank G. Shattuck passed along to his offsprings on July 23, 1934:

WHEN EVERYBODY ATE AT SCHRAFFT'S

To My Four Sons:

You ought to know, and no doubt you do know, that every good or foolish thing you do comes back to you. If you are very agreeable and sociable and have a pleasant time, your friends will be pleased to see you and you will have more or less social enjoyment.

However, the first thing in your life is to have good health, and the next thing is your job. Your job is just what you make it. If you take great interest in your work, if you accept responsibility, if you look after details and know where you are, if you keep your head, have courage and some little vision, imagination and persistence, you will be very successful, you will make more of your job, and your job will make more of you. All successful men in this country have pursued this line of action. In other words, whatever you put in, you will get out—no more, no less.

As a comparison: Mr. Jones lives in a nice little town. He is very careful and saving and is always thinking about the future as well as the present. At the end of the year Mr. Jones and his wife can say to themselves, "We have saved so much and we are so much ahead. Our house has been clean, pleasant and harmonious, and we are living happily. We do not have so many friends, perhaps, or go to many places, but we are living within our income and are very much encouraged."

Another man in this town is Mr. Smith. He has a home and a very nice family, but the Smith family is not quite so saving. Their income is five times that of the Jones family, but at the end of the year they have saved nothing. They are in debt to some extent. They have gone places and done things, but they have not thought much about economy. So, you see, the Jones family is better off than the Smith family.

It does not make so much difference what a young man gets in wages as what he makes out of his business. How well off he is financially and physically is a matter of what he saves. It depends upon harmony and the way things are done. Every man must have a job in order to live and look after his family and be comfortable and happy. This means taking responsibility and being more interested in his job than anything else. It means being careful and saving. You are all on your own. The future depends upon yourself. It is a serious matter, and I hope you will give it your very careful attention.

I thought this was the best possible advice I could give you—or anybody else.

Yours,
(signed) FGS

And here's a more lighthearted note from Frank M. on February 3, 1939. Unlike his father, he remained in Syracuse where the first store serving full meals was launched. (It was promoted as a tea garden, a quaintzy-daintzy image that took some time to erase.)

WHEN EVERYBODY ATE AT SCHRAFFT'S

Advertising Manager,
The Syracuse Journal,
Syracuse, N. Y.

Dear Sir:

With this reservation for a quarter page advertisement in your 100th Anniversary Issue, would you also accept one of the same size for your 200th Anniversary Issue? I don't think I am too optimistic for either of us in doing this, because the Journal and Schrafft's were both founded on sound American ideas.

Our restaurant here, as you probably know, is the first Schrafft's. My father started it in 1906. It's difficult to sum up his idea in a phrase, but this is very close to it: "American home cooking." And that, as he practiced it thirty-three years ago and as we practice it today, means—food at its finest . . . prepared in spic-and-span kitchens . . . in home portions . . . from American recipes.

But, as my father used to say, "You can't describe it adequately. You've got to try it to fully appreciate it." That it is appreciated is evidenced, I think, by the number of Schrafft's today—48 in all, in Syracuse, New York, Boston and Philadelphia.

At this time, too, I extend a cordial invitation to your Advertising Manager of 100 years hence to dine at Schrafft's. I am wondering now just what there will be on the menu. Customs change, and while our fundamental idea at Schrafft's does not change, we keep abreast of the times. This winter, for instance, we inaugurated the very well received Sunday Night Buffet Supper. Just what 2039 has in store for us, I can't guess. I hope not food in capsules. Somehow that never could be as satisfying as tender juicy charcoal broiled steak . . . or creamy-rich strawberry ice cream . . . or fried chicken, Maryland.

Congratulations to the Journal on its 100th Anniversary— and may it have a most prosperous second century!

Cordially yours,

(signed) F. M. Shattuck

HOW SCHRAFFT'S HELPED THEIR HELP

ONE OF THE first firms to hire women as managers, Schrafft's was an early advocate of establishing good employee relationships. Virtually unheard of in the old days, the company under Gerald Shattuck's leadership designed a profit-sharing plan for what was at one point 7700 employees. As a result, hundreds stayed for twenty-five years and some for almost fifty years. Nonetheless, help-wanted ads were constantly placed to attract additional help for full-time positions as waitresses, cooks, bakers, cashiers, sales girls, and hostesses. "No experience necessary. Meals and uniforms furnished. Paid vacations."

Another unique advantage for female employees at that time were the pregnancy benefits. Expectant mothers received monthly letters of advice and a complete layette on the infant's arrival. For the next twelve months, the new mom was sent mailings about child care and was given *a full year's leave of absence* (but without pay).

As always, service with a smile.
Illustration by T. R. Nimen

Through the house organ, *Schrafft's News, Home Style,* the top brass and even the lowliest employees were brought close to each other. This bonding, and the sense of job security and glow of good fellowship that went with it, goes a long way to explain how the staff could continually put on such a happy face.

Menus and Memorabilia From Way Back When

THANKS GO TO Eileen Markey for the following goodies. She is a daughter of the late Raymond J. Markey, a Schrafft's executive V.P. who was elected president of the New York State Restaurant Association.

JUNE 11, 1926, NOVEMBER 1, 1926

CLEARLY, THE SIMPLICITY of the food in the early days was a reflection of Frank G. Shattuck's taste. The two luncheon menus from 1926 are good examples. But if you look closely, you'll note that Schrafft's was already adding quirky touches to the food. What, for instance, was in Asparagus Tip Surprise? Or Pear Surprise, for that matter? And what was Currant Jelly doing with Roast Stuffed Shoulder of Veal?

Breads

Vanilla Muffins	.20	Bran Muffins	.20
Toast Sticks	.10	Bran Bread	.15
French Rolls	.10	Dry or Buttered Toast	.15
Nut Bread			.25

Desserts

Orange Temptation
Fresh Strawberry Cream Pie
Caramel Marshmallow Layer Cake ... .30
Apple Tart with Whipped Cream ... .30
...ake ... .25
...llop with Whipped Cream Sauce ... .25
...arian Cream ... .15
...p Custard with Cream ... .30
...n Whip ... .25
...with Roquefort Cheese ... .25
...ed Strawberry Shortcake ... .30
...arb Pie ... .35
...colate Ice Cream Cake ... .40
...Shortcake ... .25
...kies ... .50
...Cheese ... .25
... .25   a la Mode ... .15
...er Cake ... .20
... .40
... .20

Fruits

...ries with Cream ... .30
... .40
... .30   with Cream ... .25
... .25
... .35

Sundaes

	.25	Maple Pecan	.25
	.25	Fresh Pineapple	.25
	.25	Hot Caramel Almond	.25
	.25	Waldorf	.25

Beverages

	.15	Frosted Strawberry	.25
	.30	Orangeade	.30
	.25	White Rock	.25
...Dry	.30	Ginger Ale, Delatour	.25
...Milk			.20
...Milk			.30
...Buttermilk			.15

Coffee, Chocolate
...ed Chocolate ... .2.
...) .20   Serv...
... .15   Coff...
...on, English Bre...

Soups

Old Fashioned Clam Chowder	.25
Chicken Consomme	.20

Relishes

Pepper Hash			.15
Fruit Cocktail	.25	Sweet Pickles	.10
Cold Slaw	.20	Sliced Tomatoes	.25

Entrees

Fresh Lobster Fricassee with Biscuit	1.25
Chicken Croquettes with Sauce a la Schrafft and New Peas	.85
Scalloped Halibut	.55
Fried Ham Hawaiian	.65
Baked Macaroni and Cheese with Tomato Sauce	.45
Creamed Chicken on Toast	.65
Chicken Patty	.75

Salads

Cold Stuffed Egg with Potato Salad and Sliced Tomato	.85
Fresh Shrimp Salad	.85
Bartlett Pear and Cream Cheese	.60
Hearts of Lettuce with Chiffonade Dressing	.50
Asparagus Tip Surprise	.60
Fresh Greens with Beet and Egg	.50
... .35 with Cold Cuts	.85
Potato Salad	.60
Chopped Chicken and Vegetable Salad	
... .40 Vegetable Salad	.50
Egg Salad	.50
Chicken Salad ... 1.00 Fruit Salad	.50

Sandwiches
* Made with Mayonnaise

*Fresh Lobster Salad Toast Sandwich			.75
Nut Bread with Fig and Cream Cheese			.40
Bran Bread with Peanut Butter and Chili Sauce			.30
*Graham Bread with Egg and Green Pepper			.25
*Whole Wheat Gluten Bread, Chicken Liver and Bacon			.55
Rye Bread with Roquefort and Cream Cheese			.35
Sandwich a la Schrafft	.20	Pimento and Cheese	.20
*Sliced Tongue	.30	*Sliced Ham	.20
*Hot Club	.75	Supreme	.25
*Combination	.30	*Chicken Salad Sandwich	.40
*Sliced Chicken	.45	*Lettuce and Egg	.20

THE SCHRAFFT'S STORES
FRANK G. SHATTUCK COMPANY

Luncheon
Service
11 to 3

Sandwiches
*Made with Mayonnaise
*Chicken Giblet and Chopped Bacon Toast Sandwich ... .35
Nut Bread with Fig and Cream Cheese ... .40
*Whole Wheat Gluten Bread with Sliced Tongue ... .35
and Green Pepper ... .30
*Bran Bread with Walnut and Pimento ... .35
Rye Bread with Roquefort and Cream Cheese ... .25
*Graham Bread with Olive and Egg ... .20   Lettuce and Egg ... .20
*Sliced Ham Sandwich ... .75   *Chopped Ham ... .20
*Hot Club ... .45   *Sliced Tongue ... .30
*Sliced Chicken

Desserts
Tutti Frutti Meringue Glace ... .40
Almond Farina Pudding with Ice Cream Sauce ... .25
Chocolate Whipped Cream Layer Cake ... .20
Custard Pie ... .25
Hot Raspberry Tart with Whipped Cream ... .25
Apple Whip ... .25
Pineapple Dainties ... .20
Cream Cup Cake ... .15
Assorted Cookies ... .15
Lady Fingers ... .25
Hot Fudge Shortcake ... .40
Toasted Crackers with Cream Cheese and
    Preserved Strawberries ... .50
Butterscotch Ice Cream Cake ... .20
Scotch Shortbread ... .20
Crullers with Cheese ... .40
Apple Pie ... .25   a la Mode ... .20
Chocolate Layer Cake

Fruits
Preserved Figs (Individual) ... .30
Stewed Prunes ... .20
Apple Sauce ... .20   with Cream ... .20
Baked Apple ... .25
Fresh Pineapple ... .25

Ice Cream
Coffee ... .25
Vanilla ... .25
Chocolate ... .25
Frozen Pudding ... .25

Sundaes
Raspberry 'Mallow ... .25
Hot Caramel Pecan ... .25
Hot Fudge Almond ... .25
Waldorf ... .25

Beverages
Fresh Pineapple Soda ... .25
Coffee Malted Milk ... .25
Ginger Ale, Canada Dry ... .15
Individual Buttermilk ... .15
Fresh Fruit Orangeade ... .30
Chocolate Soda ... .25
Individual Sweet Milk ... .15

1424 Broadway

Monday, Nov. 1, 1926

The SCHRAFFT'S Shops
FRANK G. SHATTUCK COMPANY

New York
106 FIFTH AVENUE
907 MADISON AVENUE
141 WEST 42d STREET, near BROADWAY
1341/2 WEST 42d STREET, near BROADWAY
32 EAST 42nd STREET, near FIFTH AVENUE
16-18 EAST 42d STREET, near FIFTH AVENUE
500 BROADWAY, near WALL STREET
181 FIFTH AVENUE, at 59th STREET
22 WEST 9th STREET, near FIFTH AVENUE
5 EAST 39th STREET, near FIFTH AVENUE
68 EAST 59th STREET, near FIFTH AVENUE
11 WEST 9th STREET, near FIFTH AVENUE
23 EAST 39th STREET, near FIFTH AVENUE
31 WEST 59th STREET, near FIFTH AVENUE
51 WEST 59th STREET, near SIXTH AVENUE
32 WEST 23d STREET, near SIXTH AVENUE
69 BROAD STREET, near WALL STREET
50 BROADWAY, at CORTLANDT STREET
25 LIBERTY STREET, near BROADWAY
80 BROADWAY, at CORTLANDT STREET
21 NASSAU STREET
36 NEW STREET
43-47 MAIDEN LANE

Brooklyn
516 FULTON STREET
591 FULTON STREET

Syracuse
418-424 SOUTH WARREN STREET

Soups
...ery ... .25
...p a la Schrafft ... .20

Relishes
... .15   Queen Olives ... .15
...ery ... .25   Sliced Tomatoes ... .25
... .25

Entrees
...Sandwich ... 1.00
... Gratin ... .50
...ery Pie ... .65
...h Rice ... .45
...acon and 1 Egg .30   with 2 Eggs ... 1.35
...m on Toast ... .65
...(min.) .60   Chicken Patty ... .65   .75

Plate Dishes
...lder of Veal with Currant Jelly and
...otatoes ... .90
...th Glace Sweet Potato and New Peas ... 1.35
...ner ... .65
...shed Potatoes and Creamed Carrots ... 1.00

Potatoes
... .25   Pan Roast Potatoes ... .20
... Baked Idaho Potato ... .25

Fresh Vegetables
... .30   Buttered Beets ... .25
... .20   Creamed Cauliflower ... .30
... .25   Fresh String Beans ... .25

Salads
...gus Tips ... .60
... .45
... .55
... .50
...egetable Salad ... .60
...Cold Cuts ... .65
... .95
... 1.00
... Vegetable Salad ... .40   .50

Breads
Vanilla Muffins ... .20   Bran Muffins ... .20
French Rolls ... .10   Nut Bread ... .25
Dry or Buttered Toast ... .15   Bran Bread ... .15
Toast Sticks ... .10

Tea, Coffee, Chocolate, Etc.
Hot Chocolate (Luxuro) ... .15   Coffee (per cup) ... .15
Coffee with Cream (per pot) .20   Served for two ... .30
Tea, single service ... .20   Served for two ... .30
Orange Pekoe, Ceylon, English Breakfast, Oolong

TO DINE AT Schrafft's on Christmas day of 1933 must have been a difficult splurge for many people since it was at the height of the Depression. This could explain why in addition to the a la carte menu, a $1.25 dinner was offered that ran to five courses. While still pricey to the down-and-out, to some it may have been worth starving the rest of the week!

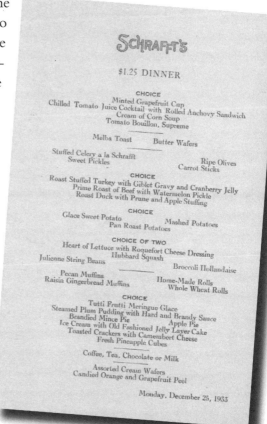

SCHRAFFT'S

$1.25 DINNER

CHOICE

Chilled Tomato Juice Cocktail with Rolled Anchovy Sandwich
Minted Grapefruit Cup
Cream of Corn Soup
Tomato Bouillon, Supreme

Melba Toast   Butter Wafers

Stuffed Celery a la Schrafft
Sweet Pickles   Ripe Olives
                                        Carrot Sticks

CHOICE

Roast Stuffed Turkey with Giblet Gravy and Cranberry Jelly
Prime Roast of Beef with Watermelon Pickle
Roast Duck with Prune and Apple Stuffing

CHOICE

Glace Sweet Potato   Mashed Potatoes
              Pan Roast Potatoes

CHOICE OF TWO

Heart of Lettuce with Roquefort Cheese Dressing
Julienne String Beans   Hubbard Squash
                                  Broccoli Hollandaise

Pecan Muffins
Raisin Gingerbread Muffins   Home-Made Rolls
                                  Whole Wheat Rolls

CHOICE

Tutti Frutti Meringue Glace
Steamed Plum Pudding with Hard and Brandy Sauce
Brandied Mince Pie   Apple Pie
Ice Cream with Old Fashioned Jelly Layer Cake
Toasted Crackers with Camembert Cheese
Fresh Pineapple Cubes

Coffee, Tea, Chocolate or Milk

Assorted Cream Wafers
Candied Orange and Grapefruit Peel

Monday, December 25, 1933

JUNE 23, 1939

WHEN THE 1939 World's Fair arrived in the New York area, Schrafft's pulled out all the stops. They wrapped the menu in a beautiful, blue cover design—with a lighthearted but persuasive message to the world of Fair visitors on the back. The choice of dishes was, of course, not international in flavor, but rather a lengthy introduction to what Frank G. Shattuck would call American home cooking. While you may not know of any home where Old Fashioned Chicken Shortcake with Spiced Peaches was cooked, nearly all of the luncheon suggestions sound enticing. And here at last is the Chopped Egg Sandwich (for 20¢ in 1939) that later became such a hit.

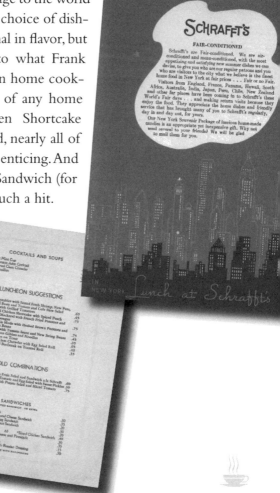

Edna St. Vincent Millay once wrote, "I love America, they give you the matches free." Well, those days are practically gone. Here, however, is a Schrafft's matchbook cover out of the smoke-filled past.

Another Schrafft's newsletter, called *Around The Town,* reported some amusing events. Here's a fun one:

"When Mrs. Terhune of Tiffany's called recently to borrow a dummy birthday cake for a table setting display, she told us they frequently used Schrafft's candy and cakes in their table settings. She added that the candy and cakes had a way of disappearing from the tables and had to be constantly replenished. Recently, in desperation, to keep a tea setting looking at its best they resorted to actually gluing the Schrafft's cupcakes to the glass plate on which they were arranged. Customers, she said, complained bitterly, saying 'This is ridiculous. You glue down the cakes and here's all this silver and china loose on the table!' But experience has taught Tiffany's that the customer who wouldn't dream of touching the luxurious Tiffany merchandise, finds Schrafft's candy and cake an irresistable temptation."

Not just the sweet treats but all the food got more and more tempting as the years rolled by. Here is one of the dozens of poultry dishes that kept customers smiling. And if you'll pardon the pun, if corn on the cob was served on the side, it had customers grinning from ear to ear. The chicken à la king is adapted from a Schrafft's recipe that appeared in the Syracuse, NY *Herald American*. The dish was remembered as one of the most popular dinner items.

SCHRAFFT'S CHICKEN À LA KING

½ cup (1 stick) unsalted butter
½ cup flour
2 cups chicken broth
½ cup heavy cream
¼ cup milk
2 egg yokes, slightly beaten
2 cups cooked chicken, skinned, boned and cut in strips
1 cup sliced mushrooms, sauteed in butter
salt & pepper to taste
½ cup pimento, thin-sliced in strips

1. Melt butter in a large saucepan. Add flour, blending the mixture.
2. Heat broth. Slowly add it and the cream and milk to the flour mixture, stirring constantly. Cook for 5 minutes on low heat.

3. Stir in the other ingredients and cook for 2 minutes.

Served on toast or in patty shells, the chicken à la king was at once attractive and tasty. The dainty shells sound very Schrafft's, but could be difficult to find. Spooning this luscious stuff on a bed of rice might be a better idea. Serves 4 with small enough portions to leave room for one of those big desserts.

Firsthand Reports

FROM AUTHOR AND EDITOR *Helen Gurley Brown:*

Arriving as a country girl from Los Angeles in New York in 1963, one had heard of things you were supposed to *do* in this great big city—museums, Empire State Building, get yourself over to Bloomingdale's and Bergdorf Goodman, show up at a Broadway show, *and* eat at Schrafft's.

Well, mercifully, this establishment had several locations in New York and I found one not far from our apartment, which I showed up in as often as possible. Sometimes David and I would find one in *another* neighborhood and have lunch. I also did mainlining on the cookie and pastry offerings. To this *day* I don't remember anything tasting better!

Yes, many of us were *devastated* to lose this culinary treasure—couldn't you get them to open up again?

FROM SYNDICATED GOSSIP COLUMNIST *Liz Smith*

Schrafft's!!!??? Where did it go? How did it get away? How welcoming it was, with its WASPy, homey comfort food. How well I remember the cheese bread and the fabulous desserts. When I became homesick for Texas I would go to Schrafft's and make myself feel better. In the sixties there were always old folks in Schrafft's at 5 P.M. having their evening Manhattans and Old Fashioneds. I guess we didn't deserve Schrafft's; fate seems to have taken it away. But it was my home away from home for many years. Thanks be to Joan Kanel Slomanson for bringing it back in all its glory.

In a footnote to her terrific book, *Dishing: Great Dish—and Dishes—from America's Most Beloved Gossip Columnist,* Liz Smith says "I don't think many people drink old-fashioneds these days. The combo of bourbon, bitters, sugar, crushed orange slice, and a maraschino cherry seems hopelessly old-fashioned." As to the Manhattans those seniors were drinking at Schrafft's, Liz found them "even more old-fashioned." Nonetheless, see page 80 for the actual, age-old recipe.

FROM FILM CRITIC *Rex Reed*

"When I first arrived in New York, fresh out of the Deep South and green as swamp grass, my idea of sophistication was to sit at the counter of Schrafft's in a Brooks Brothers polo coat, nibbling a white-chicken sandwich on cheese toast, and sipping one of Cole Porter's perfect rye old-fashioneds. Schrafft's was the ginger-peachiest part of a much-lamented lost era of nicer people, simpler values, rent-controlled apartments, and affordable menus that made Manhattan such a cool place to explore. It's the place where everybody in J. D. Salinger stories hung out on their way to foreign films. When it all ended, so did most of my enthusiasm and all of my innocence. There will never again be anything like Schrafft's."

FROM *Helen Slate*

A SCHRAFFT'S HOSTESS WITH THE MOSTEST

WHEN A BEAUTIFUL young woman named Helen, as tall and statuesque as a model, came to the Schrafft's employment office on 23rd Street in search of a waitressing job, she was turned down. Why? Because they were more interested in immediately moving her up to the loftier position of hostess.

The year was 1943, there was a war on, and Schrafft's needed attractive, personable help to keep business up to speed. Helen Beebe, who later became Helen Slate, was a natural. Her own mother, Esther Sullivan Beebe, had been a Schrafft's waitress 25 years earlier. By coincidence, at the Fifth Avenue/46th Street store where Helen was sent, the head hostess named Irene Winterbottom had been a waitress with Helen's mother. Like so many Schrafft's employees, Irene had stayed on and on, as did a Mr. Kelly. A busboy way-back-when, he worked his way up to store manager of the store where Helen hostessed.

That particular store was a five-story extravaganza. You can see a picture of the splendid facade in Chapter 6. Swanky as all get-out, the place had a different ambience on each of the dining floors. According to Helen, the topmost floor, to which she didn't succeed, had a colonial décor and to complement the setting, the hostesses were required to wear long gowns. On her floor, hostesses had to wear ladylike black-and-white or navy-and-white, street-length clothes. Her tweed skirt did not conform, so she raced up and down Fifth Avenue to find appropriate apparel before starting work.

Helen reports that the head hostess was everyone's teacher who laid down the law according to Schrafft's. Like the waitresses, the appearance of each hostess had to pass daily inspection. Moreover, Irene Winterbottom would sit down at a table and act as if she were a customer, showing the hostesses exactly how to treat people. The rules were rigid. *Everything* had to be done the Schrafft's way. (Helen cited as an extreme example: the spoon served with a soda had to be positioned so the liquid from the spigot wouldn't hit the ice cream.) Despite all the dictum, Helen says she loved working at Schrafft's and still has fond memories of it sixty years later.

But a hostess's main job was, of course, seating customers. Helen explains that one hostess would be stationed at the entrance and another would be out on the floor. When seats and tables became available, the floor hostess would hold up the number of fingers that indicated how many places were free. They would also have to make sure that the tables were cleared and then set up again in an expeditious way.

If this all seems easy as pie, one wonders why today's hostesses can't be trained to work this way. Instead, as one restaurant critic put it, "they act so arrogant and ignorant, you want to hit them with an axe."

To quote ANNE OLIVER, a customer in the good old days: "Everyone was so sweet and so polite. Even if the place was crowded, the dedicated hostesses knew how to handle people. They would say, 'Please be patient. We'll have a table for you in no time.' I miss Schrafft's because there are no places like that anymore."

FROM *June Springer:*

1. June Springer remembers that when she and her sister were preteens, their mother allowed them to take the Blue Bus from their town, Bogota, New Jersey, to New York City. "There were many caveats involved," June recalls. "We were allowed to go to any of the big movie houses (The Paramont or The Capitol or The Strand) and then we could go to Schrafft's—and *only* Schrafft's—for our treat: lunch at best or perhaps an ice cream. Nothing tasted better. Finally, all smiles, we would walk the few blocks south to the Blue Bus and home."

2. Fast-forward a few years to when June started making the rounds or auditioning or even working in a show. "Where," she asks, "did we young actors invariably end up discussing The Theatre and our role in it? The very same Schrafft's! It was our place."

3. Then June married John Springer, the veteran publicist who represented such talents as Marilyn Monroe, Judy Garland, Gary Cooper, Montgomery Clift, Gene Kelly, Grace Kelly, Bette Davis, Richard Burton, Elizabeth Taylor, and Henry Fonda, to name just a few of the many. After a Broadway show, where did the stars come out at night? You guessed it. "Everyone headed for the Schrafft's in the theatre district," June reports.

WHEN EVERYBODY ATE AT SCHRAFFT'S

FROM *Joe Franklin,* THE KING OF NOSTALGIA

THE SELF-PROCLAIMED "Wizard of Woz" is a gold mine of information about New York's past and naturally has a story to tell about Schrafft's. Dreaming of the days when New York was the best of all places to see the big vaudeville stars perform, Joe Franklin had as his personal matinée idol Al Jolson. Even as a child, Franklin rated Jolson as the world's greatest entertainer. He says he still does, but no slouch himself as an entertainer, Franklin had his first of many radio shows at age fourteen and hoped to interview Jolson for his high school newspaper.

Someone sent Joe on a fool's errand looking for Al Jolson at the Martha Washington. It turned out to be a hotel for women only. He finally tracked down his hero at the Sherry Netherlands where his other favorite performer, Eddie Cantor, also stayed when in town. After granting Franklin an interview, Jolson was so impressed that someone so young admired his work, he invited Franklin to have dinner with him and his manager. The restaurant of choice: the nearby Schrafft's at Madison Avenue and 58th Street.

Franklin recalls that Jolson liked the bread so much, he ate loads of it spread with lots of butter before the food he ordered arrived. When Joe precociously asked why he selected Schrafft's over such restaurants as Lindy's and Longchamps, Jolson said he was very choosy. Using an exaggerated Brooklyn "a" he said, "I like Shee-r*aaaa*fft's because it's so cl*aaaa*sy!"

When Joe Franklin grew up (total height: 5 ft. 5 in.) and acquired a measure of fame of his own, he often held court at Schrafft's between bites of his favorite sandwiches. Two admittedly corny jokes that he claims to this day came from Al Jolson: (1) When he went to some restaurant and exclaimed, "I'm so hungry, I could eat a horse," the waiter said "You've come to the right place." (2) When they passed that other chain restaurant, Childs, and saw a sign that said "Childs Bar," Jolson asked if that was legal.

FROM *Professor Irwin Corey,* THE DEAN OF DOUBLETALK

FOR ONCE, THE words of that remarkable humorist, Professor Irwin Corey, need no translation, but his story is nonetheless amusing. "When I was a young man I would deliver lunchtime sandwiches, not for Schrafft's but for a drugstore," says Professor Corey, "On the way, I would pass the Schrafft's at Fifth Avenue and 13th Street. The name stuck with me and some years later, when I won a trip to Europe in a raffle, I came across it again in Paris.

"I took my wife, my sister-in-law, and her husband to a restaurant that claimed to be *Cuisine Domestique Á La Schrafft's.*" It sounds as if they meant it to mean they served home-cooked American-style dishes, but Corey says that the food and everything else about the place was very French and very fancy though there was a table of good-looking girls from Texas next to them. Naturally, he joked around with the young ladies, which didn't go over big with the English-speaking management. Then, since Corey wasn't wearing a necktie, the waiter lent him one, but wouldn't let him put it on at the table. He insisted on escorting Corey to the restroom to outfit him.

FROM *Jeanne Leo,* FORMER AIRLINE STEWARDESS

AN IOWA FARM girl who flew the friendly skies of United, Jeanne Burns Leo didn't discover Schrafft's until her flight from San Francisco landed in Boston in 1956. Unprepared for what she came to know as the stuffy Boston society of the time, she sashayed into Schrafft's one summer day wearing a pair of shorts. To her surprise, the place was filled to overflowing with ladies dressed to the nines. Hats, gloves, jewels—all their finery was on display. Needless to say, young Miss Burns received a cool reception. No air conditioning needed. So she sat at the counter, quickly sipped a soda, and left.

Later, when she was married, Jeanne and her spouse used her flying privileges to visit Egypt. When they looked up an old acquaintance there, Dr. Ragab, who had come to Boston to go to medical school, he regaled them with his own Schrafft's tale. New to New England and unprepared for the freezing winter weather, he had sought advice on how to keep warm. A friend suggested that he get some earmuffs. "Earmuffs? Muffs?" he asked. "Yeah, that's right, muffs," he was told, "They sell them at many stores around here." So, with a look of confusion on his face, Ragab went out in the cold and the first store he checked out was, you guessed it, a Schrafft's.

His request for muffs puzzled the clerk, but she suggested that perhaps what he meant were muffins, English muffins. Nobody could be more puzzled than he when she handed two of them to him, but he politely tried to put one on each ear. Of course, anyone within earshot assumed that he was some kind of a clown or a nutcase. Giving back the muffins, he was able to purchase ear-muffs, inedible but wearable ones, in the store next door.

FROM *Alvin Mass,* ATTORNEY-AT-LAW

NOT ALL THAT long ago, Al Mass owned a Manhattan restaurant, but his story about Schrafft's goes back some forty-five years. When he was fresh out of law school, an assemblyman called and asked him to attend an arraignment at Criminal Court. He sought Mass's help in a case where the young son from a prominent Pittsburgh banking family was charged with attempted assault and attempted murder.

According to the kid, he had fallen for an Irish waitress at Schrafft's. Overwhelmed by her beauty, but unable to get to first base with her, he dreamed up a scheme to get her attention and win her admiration. To wit, he would hire a hit man to do some minor bodily harm to her, such as breaking one of her legs. Nothing serious, mind you, but enough to land her in the hospital. Then, in his pipe dream, he would visit her constantly, bringing her not only flowers, but a television set and other great gifts.

As luck or unluck would have it, the so-called hit man whom he met at a bar turned out to be an undercover cop, hence the arrest. Before the case was to come to trial in the hands of some big-time law firm hired by the family, Mass got the kid temporarily transferred to a neurological institute. The family members were so grateful, they took Mass to the Harvard Club and rewarded him with more money than he had ever earned before.

Now if only the waitresses at Schrafft's hadn't been so good looking . . . !

FROM *Carmela Cicero Maresca,* MARKETING CONSULTANT

Ms. Maresca reports: Like so many boys and girls, Schrafft's was the destination restaurant when my grand-mother took me out to eat. And some years later, when I lived near a Schrafft's in New York's East Seventies, it was where I took my young son for a snack or a sweet. In Schrafft's you got the feeling that the people working there were restaurant careerists. What they were doing was what they wanted to do. The waitresses behaved as if they were part of the Schrafft's family, which in a way they were. Any day, any time, they gave you a warm welcome and treated you almost like royalty.

Today, you are often served, or ill-served, by gum-chewing, lackadaisical people too busy talking to each other to bother with customers. The job and you mean little to them unless you're in a restaurant so expensive, the waiters are anticipating huge tips. Of course, even in the old days, there were some would-be actors and actresses keeping body and soul together by working at Schrafft's, but I think it's more common in cafes today. Have you heard the one about the customer asking the waiter, "Are you an actor?" "Yes," he replies with a proud look on his face. "Well then," says the customer, "Do you think you could act like a waiter tonight?"

FROM *Reva Fox,* AN EARLY TEA-MAKER OF THE METROPOLITAN OPERA

BEFORE THE HEARTLESS demolition in 1966 of the elegant old Metropolitan Opera house, Reva Fox worked there for the legendary manager, Rudolf Bing. As his right-hand woman, one of her assignments was the brewing of the tea. To eat with it, Mr. Bing, as Mrs. Fox called him (he had not yet been knighted) always brought his lunch from home in a brown paper bag—and brought the empty bag back home. Unlike the boss, the staff members did not always eat in. The opera house stretched from Broadway to Seventh Avenue, and Reva Fox remembers joining her cohorts for lunch at a nearby Schrafft's.

"I hardly ever deviated from my order," Mrs. Fox says, "invariably having an omelet or scrambled eggs, crisp bacon, and a fabulous baked apple. Part of the enjoyment came from the welcoming atmosphere, the wood-paneled interior, and pleasant service which made every visit a special occasion."

Living at 73rd Street and Third Avenue, Mrs. Fox visited another Schrafft's once a week. After breakfast and before going to work she would stop there just for the pleasure of downing their "yummy, fresh-squeezed grapefruit juice." What she probably didn't know was that glass after glass of Schrafft's grapefruit juice was the morning-after drink of choice (along with hairs of the dog) of men trying to cure their hangovers

Schrafft's was even part of the picture when Reva Fox found the man who was "the perfect lifetime companion." What proof did she have that her future husband was the one? He always took her to Schrafft's after a movie so she could have a coffee soda while he had a "black and white." They never deserted Schrafft's, but continued the custom until, like the old Met Opera house, Schrafft's deserted them.

Who's Who in the Kitchen?

IN THE BRITISH TV series, "Fawlty Towers," a guest asked to cancel an order of so-called fresh fruit salad and was told, "Oh I'm sorry; chef has already opened the tin." This would never have happened at a Schrafft's.

Jokes aside, at Schrafft's the customers came first. And anyway, there were no chefs, just cooks . Today, on the one hand, we have battalions of anonymous hash-slingers in fast food chains, while in the white tablecloth outposts, celebrity chefs reign supreme. Unlike most restaurants before and after the Schrafft's era, at all the stores women cooks ruled the roost. Frank G. Shattuck started the tradition seeing it as the best way to replicate home-cooked family meals. As testament to the success of this approach, according to *Real Life at the White House* by John Whitcomb, Eleanor Roosevelt was so dissatisfied with her chief cook, Henrietta Nesbitt, and so enamored with Schrafft's, she sent Mrs. Nesbitt to New York City to spend a few days in one of the restaurant kitchens. (Mrs. N. probably felt right at home there amidst the women, but one wonders how much the White House food improved after her cooking lesson.)

At Schrafft's, cooks were under orders to follow instructions to the letter. As the old recipe cards show, everything was spelled out in advance, written in stone, so to speak—ingredients, exact portion sizes, and even the arrangement of food on the plate. Any individual creativity was stifled in the name of a consistency that customers came to appreciate. If you had grown fond of a certain dish, the popular chicken à la king, for example, the last thing you wanted was for some imaginative cook to replace the mushrooms with artichoke bottoms. Nonetheless, the powers that be did update many recipes through the years and also provide many variations on the favorite themes. There were any number of different chowders, pot pies, chicken dishes, and so on and so forth.

A DOWNSTAIRS STORY

DOROTHEA HERZ RABKIN and her husband Leo are avid collectors who have donated their treasures to the Museum of American Folk Art. In a telephone conversation, Mrs. Rabkin painted a verbal picture of what it was like to be an underling in the kitchen at the Times Square Schrafft's. A refugee from Nazi Germany, fresh off the boat in 1949 and in need of a job, she wanted to stay at Schrafft's until she would feel more secure with the English language. Sad to say, she was laughed at because of the way she spoke and given menial tasks. But she says that in all fairness, she really enjoyed the food. Before breakfast, lunch, and dinner the staff would have a taste-testing, after which she was always invited to sit down and eat.

A DEPRESSING DEPRESSION REPORT

IN 1935, BEFORE displaced persons from World War II like Dorothea Rabkin landed on U.S. shores, the nation was still in the throes of the Depression. New York streets overflowed with beggars, bag ladies, pushcarts, pickpockets and in short, all manner of ne'er-do-wells trying desperately to survive.

Earnings and consequently wages were unbelievably low, yet fearing any kind of governmental control, hotel and restaurant owners continued to block state legislation that would establish even a miniscule minimum wage. It may sound laughable to you now, but a specially convened wage board was recommending 18 cents an hour to table-service waitresses and 27 cents an hour to non-service food workers such as those in the kitchen. The assumption there seemed to be that unlike the other employees, waitresses made "big money" in tips, but an industry spokesman admitted that "there are few tips paid these days."

The three representatives from the hotel and restaurant industry on the wage board were Francis Gorman, manager of the Hotel Astor and vice-president of the New York State Hotel Association; Charles A. Laube, president of the National Restaurant Association and director of the Buffalo Restaurant Association (Laube restaurants were big in Buffalo); and George R. LeSauvage, assistant to the president of Frank G. Shattuck and Company. Three generations of the LeSauvage family worked their way up at Schrafft's, one of them rising to the post of executive vice-president.

A story in the New York *World-Telegram* claimed that waitresses in the Schrafft's stores were required to write letters protesting the passage of the proposed minimum wage. John Shattuck, vice-president of the Frank G. Shattuck Company, insisted that such letters were unauthorized and that Schrafft's would be in favor of a minimum wage for women. LeSauvage didn't sign the wage board's report, but unlike other companies in the hotel and restaurant industry, Schrafft's didn't deduct from salaries for uniforms and meals. When advertising for female workers, they made it clear that the company provides them.

The one regulation that did go into effect was the "night-work law" requiring that female restaurant workers cease their labor at 10 P.M. This might explain Schrafft's use of waiters in the evening when supper was served, and certainly all the bartenders were male.

You Say Tomato, I Say Tomahto

AS EARLY AS 1900, New York City had a great variety of eating places. There was something for everybody, whether you spoke the broken English of newly arrived immigrants or with the hoity-toity accent of the upper class. Many of the eateries charged the city's paupers mere pennies for a meal, although the years prior to World War I have been called New York's Age of Elegance when consumption by the wealthy was on a grand scale.

Certainly by the 1930s there were thousands of dining places in New York City. Where and when money was particularly scarce, one could stave off starvation at a cafeteria, soft-drink stand, or one of Horn & Hardart's popular Automats which got their start in 1903. For the more affluent, there were posh hotels like the Biltmore, Ambassador, Delmonico, St. Moritz, St. Regis, and of course, Waldorf-Astoria, offering dinner and supper dancing, often with a formal dress requirement. The well-to-do also frequented nightclubs such as El Morocco and the Stork Club as well as the Rainbow Room on the 65th floor of Rockefeller Center. Billy Rose directed a lavish nightclub called Casa Mañana on the spot where Earl Carroll had staged his glamourous *Vanities* prior to 1935. In short, the life was swell if you could afford it.

But from 1920 to 1933, Prohibition took its toll on many of the fancier, pricier restaurants. Apparently swanky restaurants like Delmonico's and Sherry's couldn't survive without the steep markup they had been able to exact on wines and spirits. On the other hand, alcoholic drinks were plentiful at zillions of speakeasies, some of which survived the period, turning into legitimate bars and restaurants. Spawned during Prohibition, speakeasies like the 21 Club in midtown and Chumley's in Greenwich Village came out of hiding, and Texas Guinan's "speak" on West 54th changed hands and names. The Brass Rail which started as a counter-only sandwich shop during Prohibition grew into a four-story restaurant seating over 1,000 people.

Gourmet dining palaces like Le Pavillon and the Spanish Pavillion came into being during the 1939 World's Fair. The Stage Deli attracts tourists to this day and Luchow's lasted from 1882 until 1982. The original Lindy's drew a crowd of sports fans, as did ex-prizefighting champ Jack

WHEN EVERYBODY ATE AT SCHRAFFT'S

Dempsey, playing host at his own Broadway restaurant. (You could often see him standing in the front window.) Keen's English Chop House is as keen as ever, renamed Keen's Steakhouse although mutton chops are still the specialty. Onion soup, frogs' legs, and *crêpes suzettes* were star attractions at numerous French bistros. And the next door neighbors, Chinatown and Little Italy, fed people on the cheap. Just as today, there were Jewish, Irish, Spanish, Swedish, Russian, Mexican, Hungarian, German, Italian, Japanese, Armenian, Austrian, and East Indian restaurants in the New York melting pot, stirring up citywide excitement.

Were there other chain restaurants besides Schrafft's in the New York City of the thirties? Yes indeed. Caruso had six branches in Manhattan, Huyler's had eleven, and Longchamps had twelve. As reported on a previous page, Schrafft's "tree" had already sprouted thirty-eight branches in the metropolitan area at the time, only outdone in size by Childs which had forty-four Manhattan branches.

WHAT MAKES SCHRAFFT'S MORE MEMORABLE? When you compare it with Longchamps and Childs, there's really no comparison. Longchamps had considerable charm, but it put on airs. It had a costly, ritzy quality, too rich for many people's blood. And then there was Childs. Childs had a wonderful come-on, a woman cooking up pancakes in the window, but in every other respect, the places looked and acted too crazy-clean. Self-promoted as hygienic restaurants, Childs garbed the help in clinical white. For all Frank G. Shattuck's emphasis on sanitation, he never let his stores look like hospitals.

After a long life, Horn & Hardart's popular Automat chain went bankrupt. As to Longchamps, Childs, and Schrafft's, they went the way of Riese, the organization that bought up all three and others, mainly for the real estate value, and then built their own empire of Manhattan eateries. But above and beyond Schrafft's rivals, the memory of the stores lingers on the longest because getting together there was a way of life unsurpassed by the competition. When you were in the mood for exotica like shashlik or gefilte fish or Peruvian sopa de camarones, or wanted to get gussied up and go dancing, you would obviously head elsewhere. Otherwise you could take your pick of the Schrafft's stores in or out of Manhattan and enjoy the relaxing experience. While some thought of it as stodgy, many more loved it for its gentility. In fact, the appeal was so great, New Yorkers and visitors from out-of-town looked upon Schrafft's as their second home.

Oh Those Sandwiches!!!

ALTHOUGH THE NEW York City Schrafft's opened in 1898, the first store serving full meals was opened in 1906 in Syracuse, New York, where Frank G. Shattuck's son, Frank M., continued to live. (Initially, this upstate store served nothing but ham and chicken sandwiches before the menu was expanded.) Of course, sandwiches never did leave Schrafft's menus and were always among the star attractions. One extreme version was described on the menu as *"Sandwich in a Dish. Sliced Breast of Turkey and Imported Ham on Toast Topped with Continental Style Cheese Sauce and a Juicy Pineapple Ring. A Meal in itself! Served with a Green Grocer Salad."*

There were also these bewitching and sometimes bewildering choices from the sandwich grill . . .

1. Grilled Special Cheddar Cheese Sandwich with Currant Jelly
2. Grilled Sliced Ham Sandwich on Cheese Bread
3. Grilled Peanut Butter, Chili Sauce and Bacon Sandwich
4. Grilled Chopped Corned Beef and Chili Sauce Sandwich
5. Grilled Deviled Shrimp and Cheese Sandwich
6. Grilled American Cheese and Tomato Sandwich
7. Grilled Special Chopped Chicken Sandwich
8. Grilled Baked Ham Sandwich with Mustard Sauce
9. Grilled Cheddar Cheese and Pimento Sandwich
10. Grilled Deviled Ham Sandwich
11. Grilled Special Tuna Fish Sandwich
12. Grilled American Cheese and Bacon Sandwich
13. Grilled Chopped Chicken Liver and Bacon Sandwich
14. Grilled Chopped Corned Beef and Swiss Cheese Sandwich
15. Grilled Deviled Ham and Swiss Cheese Sandwich

All in a day's work: a sandwich maker at the ESSO/Rockefeller Center Schrafft's.

A LOST & FOUND TREASURE: The recipe for that wonderful stuff, Schrafft's cheese bread, seemed to have died and gone to food heaven. Although the Shattuck family has the list of ingredients, a Kraft product in it called "Cheese Tang" no longer exists. In fact, people at the company today say they never even heard of it.

Here, however, is that list of the actual ingredients from 1958.

$$\frac{1}{16} = .0625 \qquad \frac{20}{10} = 2\,lbs = 2\,loaves$$

Cheese Bread Dough Preliminary		Schrafft's 10-1140 # Recalculated 5-23-58																		
PRODUCTION	10		20		30		40		50		60		70		80		90		100	**POUNDS**	
	LBS.	OZ.	LBS.	OZ.	LBS.	OZ.	LBS.	OZ.	LBS.	OZ.	LBS.	OZ.	LBS.	OZ.	LBS.	OZ.	LBS.	OZ.	LBS.	OZ.	
Water 1" 9⅛	3	3	6	7	9	10	12	14	16	-	19	-	23	-	26	-	29	-	32	-	36
Gran. Sugar 12 oz	1	2	2	7	4		5		7		8½		9¾		11½		13		14		
Salt 1 oz	2		4		5		7		9		11		13		15		1		2		
Grated Cheese 11 oz	1	5	2	9	4		5		6		7		9		10		11		12	14	
Cheese Tang		4		7			2		3		3		4		5		5		6		
Patent Flour 1" 11	5	6	10	12	16		21		27		32		38		43		48		54	-	
Yeast 3¼ oz	1		3		4½		6		7½		9		10½		12		13½		15		
Formula Wt.	10	3½	20	7	30	8½	40	12	50	15½	61	4	71	6½	81	1½	91	11½	102	6½	

DOUGLAS L. McINTYRE
Production Control
Wareham, Massachusetts

Water .59 × 16 = 9 oz = ½ cup
Sugar .25 × 16 = 120 g / 120 g = 1.71 cup

One recently published book has attempted to recreate the bread. Although it sounds very tasty, the recipe includes milk and butter which as you can see were not in the Schrafft's original. A closer facsimile of the terrific sandwich loaf (but without the sugar) plus a long French bread loaf is reprinted here. The recipe from *Knead It, Punch It, Bake It!* by Judith and Evan Jones can't be too difficult, since it's meant to be made by parents with their children.

CHEESE BREAD MADE TWO WAYS

1 package (1 scant tablespoon) active dry yeast
1¾ cups warm water
2 tsp. salt
3½ to 4½ cups white flour
1 cup grated sharp cheddar cheese
cornmeal

1. Put the yeast in a large bowl and pour ½ cup of the warm water over it. After a minute stir with your finger to make sure the yeast is dissolved.
2. Mix the remaining 1¼ cups water with the salt and pour it over the dissolved yeast. Stir in the flour, a cup at a time, and when the dough becomes hard to stir, turn it out onto a floured work surface. Let the dough rest while you clean out the bowl.

3. Scrape up the dough and knead it for 10 minutes, adding more white flour as necessary, until it is smooth and elastic.

4. Rub the cleaned bowl lightly with soft butter or vegetable oil and return the dough to it, turning to coat. Cover with plastic wrap and let rise until almost tripled in size, 2 to 3 hours.

5. Punch the risen dough down and turn it out onto the floured surface. Spread it out and sprinkle the cheese all over. Then roll the dough up and knead it just long enough to incorporate the cheese into the dough.

6. Grease an 8-inch loaf pan. Using about two-thirds of the dough, form a loaf and place it in the greased pan. Roll the remaining dough into a 10 to 12 inch long loaf and place on a baking sheet sprinkled with cornmeal. Cover each loaf with a kitchen towel and let rise until doubled in size—about 45 minutes.

7. After the bread has risen for 30 minutes, preheat the oven to 450 degrees F.

8. Place the loaves in the oven. Remove the French loaf after 18 to 20 minutes, when the top is golden. Turn down the heat to 350 degrees and let the pan loaf bake for another 10 minutes. Cool on racks. Enjoy!

This simple (and simply delicious) sandwich cries for Schrafft's special bread:

GRILLED SLICED HAM
ON CHEESE BREAD

(1964)

Butter 2 slices of cheese bread evenly on both sides. Place 1½ oz. sliced ham on bottom slice of the buttered bread. Cover with top slice of bread and grill at 400° for 2½ minutes. *Do not cut.* Serve on a heated plate.

THE EGG AND SCHRAFFT'S

MANY PEOPLE RECALL the CHOPPED EGG SAL-AD SANDWICHES WITH THE CRUSTS CUT OFF. There were many variations on this theme: chopped egg and olive, chopped egg and celery, chopped egg and dill pickle, chopped egg with chopped bacon, chopped egg with chopped green pepper, chopped egg with sliced cucumber, chopped egg with chives and tomato slices—and so on and so forth, to say nothing of the deviled, sliced, scrambled and fried egg sandwiches. High cholesterol? Who cared! All of these egg sandwiches were not only crustless, but were cut diagonally into three pieces. But the

Seventeen Sandwich (whatever that name means) takes the chopped egg to new heights.

SCHRAFFT'S SEVENTEEN SANDWICH
(SLICED HAM, CHOPPED EGG AND WATERCRESS) (1956)

2 slices of freshly toasted bread
butter
2 oz. slice of boiled ham
watercress
mayonnaise
½ cup chopped hard-boiled egg, mixed with a little mayo
paprika
olive and pickle garnish

1. Butter bottom slice of toast evenly to edges and place ham over it. Cover generously with watercress.
2. Spread mayonnaise evenly to edges of top slice of toast and place on the watercress.
3. Spread chopped egg mixture over top of sandwich with a fork. Sprinkle lightly with paprika. Cut diagonally through center.
4. Serve on hot dinner plate with cut edges turned to the outside and with corners together in center of plate.
5. On one side, on a nice nest of watercress, place one queen olive and one sweet pickle.

WHEN EVERYBODY ATE AT SCHRAFFT'S

Other Schrafft's sandwich recipes would fill a whole book, but here are a few of the many for your delectation. Note the unusual way the sandwich halves are sometimes positioned on the plates and decoratively garnished.

BACON, AVOCADO AND TOMATO SANDWICH
(1955)

2 slices of freshly toasted bread, buttered
1 avocado, peeled, cut in half lengthwise, sliced and marinated in
French dressing
4 thin (¼-inch) slices of tomato
2 strips of bacon, crisply broiled
1 crisp lettuce leaf
mayonnaise
2 radishes

1. Cover bottom slice of toast with well-drained avocado slices.
2. Place tomato slices over the avocado and the bacon over the tomato. Top with lettuce leaf.
3. Spread top slice of toast with mayonnaise and place on the lettuce. Cut diagonally through center of sandwich.
4. Serve on hot dinner plate with cut edges to the outside and corners together in center of plate.
5. Garnish with radish "roses," one on either side of sandwich.

HOT ROAST BEEF SANDWICH FOR ONE

(1925; rewritten 1955)

4 oz. (¼ lb) cooked beef left over from a roast,
and cut thickly by hand
butter and oil
leftover gravy (or fresh from a can), heated
2 slices buttered toast
French-fried onion rings

1. Place beef in a pan, dot with butter, and put a small amount of oil in the bottom of the pan to prevent burning.
2. Baste frequently while heating beef, but taking care that the meat does not become too dry and well done. Moisten with a little hot gravy.
3. Put sandwich together on buttered toast and pour more hot gravy over it.
4. Serve on hot dinner plate with a mound of French-fried onion rings—either homemade or canned.

SPECIAL JUMBO TORPEDO SANDWICH

(1955; 1959)

If you think Schrafft's only doled out small portions, this precursor to the hero sandwich will make you think again. Many of these were prepared for outgoing orders.

1 torpedo club roll
mayonnaise
2 oz. Swiss cheese, sliced thin
2 oz. bologna, sliced thin
2 oz. liverwurst, sliced thin
2 slices tomato, each ¼-inch thick
2 Tbsp. cole slaw, mixed with mayonnaise
2 tsp. sweet piccalilli relish

1. Cut roll in half lengthwise. Spread a thin coating of mayonnaise to edges of each half.
2. On bottom half, place Swiss cheese to cover roll. Place bologna on one end of roll and liverwurst on the opposite end.
3. Put one slice of tomato on top of the bologna and the other slice of tomato on the liverwurst.
4. Place cole slaw on one tomato slice and piccalilli on the other.
5. Cut sandwich in half diagonally, securing each half with a toothpick.

OPEN TUNA FISH CLUB SANDWICH

(1964)

1 slice of white bread, buttered
1 crisp lettuce leaf
3 thin slices of tomato
3 thin slices of sweet (red) onion
1 scoop tuna fish, lightly mixed with mayonnaise
6 slices of hard-boiled egg
2 anchovy filets
1 pimento-stuffed olive
½ oz. crisp potato chips

1. Cover the slice of bread with lettuce leaf. Top with tomato slices and then the onion slices.
2. Carefully spread tuna fish mixture over onions. Place egg slices, diagonally, across top of tuna fish.
3. Lay anchovy filets, crisscrossed, over egg slices. Place olive on a toothpick and stick in center of anchovies.
4. Serve on one side of cold 9-inch salad plate with potato chips on opposite side of plate.

CHOPPED CHICKEN TEA SANDWICH

(1937; rewritten 1960)

Another favorite, running a close second to the egg salad sandwiches. Here's how it was cut up and served at teatime or for takeout.

buttered white bread
1 cup finely chopped chicken
dash of cayenne
salt & pepper to taste
½ cup mayonnaise

1. Mix chicken, cayenne, salt & pepper, and mayonnaise together.
2. Spread a slightly rounded scoop of the mixture on one slice of the bread.
3. Close sandwich with another slice that has been *lightly spread* with mayonnaise.
4. Remove all crusts and cut into 4 squares.

[NOTE: Schrafft's used the mixture to make eleven tea sandwiches. You may be more generous with the portions.]

"Here's to the Ladies Who Lunch"

ANY MEMORY OF Schrafft's is incomplete without mentioning the well-dressed women in hats who dined there regularly. In the early days, the stores were little more than tearooms, with the added attraction of a soda fountain offering counter service. But as Schrafft's popularity grew, so did the stores. In Manhattan. a part of the large, lavish branch at Madison Avenue and East 58th Street was looked upon by a clique of ladies as their private club. In *Mauve Gloves & Madmen, Clutter & Vine,* Tom Wolfe describes these matrons as being all dressed up for their afternoon outings in "peach wool suits with fur trim at the collars and cuffs and hats with enormous puffed up crowns of cream-colored velvet, over apricot-colored hair."

How members of the East 58th Street lunch bunch may have looked, dressed to the nines and gobbling up the goodies.

Illustration by T. R. Nimen

The actual East 58th Street hangout of the ladies who lunched.

A typically cheerful waitress, passing the time of day and patiently taking orders.

There are, of course, status restaurants to this day, but a major difference is that the Schrafft's ladies didn't just go there to see and be seen. They actually *ate*. According to Wolfe, "The ladies' typical meal at Schrafft's was a cheeseburger, coffee, and a sundae. But such sundaes! Sundaes with towers of ice cream and nuts and sauces and fudge and maraschino cherries of a quality and buttery beauty such as the outside world has never dreamed of!" He goes on to show how expertly the waitresses catered to the whims of these fussy women, practically canonizing these helpers as angels and nurses "sent by Our Lady of Comfort." Indeed, these incredibly considerate waitresses in their black and white frocks looked and acted as if they belonged to a holy culinary order.

With or without all those extra toppings, the hot fudge sundae is remembered fondly. In a letter to the *New York Times,* a customer named Patricia Daniels praised it as "so thick, so gloriously oozy, it turned to solid candy as the ice cream puddled around it." Here, if you can't fight the temptation, is the Shattuck family's recipe for you to try.

SCHRAFFT'S HOT FUDGE SAUCE #1

1 stick (¼ lb.) unsalted butter
3 squares unsweetened chocolate
1 cup sugar
pinch of salt
1 cup heavy cream
1 tsp. vanilla extract

1. Melt butter, chocolate, and sugar in top of double boiler with very hot water in the lower part of the boiler.
2. Stir when melted, then add cream and salt and stir again. Let this cook for 2 hours in top of double boiler over hot water, taking care that the water doesn't boil out.

3. Remove from heat and stir in vanilla. Sauce thickens when it cools or when put on ice cream. Can be refrigerated. At serving time, reheat in top of double boiler over hot water.

And here is a less time-consuming, more frequently described version:

SCHRAFFT'S HOT FUDGE SAUCE #2

1 Tbsp. unsweetened cocoa
1 cup sugar
¾ cup heavy cream
¼ cup light corn syrup
2 Tbsp. butter
2 oz. unsweetened chocolate, chopped
1 tsp. vanilla
few drops malt vinegar

1. In heavy saucepan over medium heat, whisk together cocoa, sugar and ¼ cup of the heavy cream until smooth.
2. Stir in corn syrup, butter, chocolate and rest of the cream. Bring to a boil.
3. Remove from heat. Stir in vanilla and vinegar. Sauce thickens when it cools or when put on ice cream.

(For future use, refrigerate in tightly covered jar.
4. Reheat, whisking the sauce, in top of double boiler over hot water.)

See what the ladies in a Helen Hokinson's New Yorker cartoon said about such Schrafft's treats . . .

"Sometimes I think Schrafft's doesn't care about calories."

ANDY WARHOL'S WILD CONTRIBUTION. Although Schrafft's did make a low-calorie salad dressing, the rich desserts were among their main claims to fame. So much so, the company actually hired Andy Warhol at great expense in late 1968 to create a publicity-generating commercial about the ice cream sundaes. Literally stripped down for action, Warhol and his crew of actors really went wild with the colors of a dish of ice cream shooting out in all directions. *Playboy* described the commercial as "a long, voluptuous panning shot of a chocolate sundae with all of the mistakes TV can make kept in."

The product starring in this crazy light show was called "THE UNDERGROUND SUNDAE." Long gone at the time, Frank G. Shattuck would probably not have approved of the trendy underground lingo which the stores under the direction of his son Frank M. used to feature the sundae while playing up Warhol's name:

> *"Yummy Schrafft's vanilla ice cream in two groovy heaps, with mind-blowing chocolate sauce undulating within a mountain of pure whipped cream topped with a pulsating maraschino cherry served in a bowl as big as a boat—all for $1.10."*

On the other hand, when the lady's lunch bunch was determined to watch their weight, they might have picked at this mélange of mixed fruit, a somewhat psychedelic experience in its own right. Enjoy it!

SCHRAFFT'S COMBINATION FRUIT PLATE

(1933; rewritten 1957)

1. Peel and slice fresh pineapple in ½-inch slices; re-move core and cut in inch pieces, cutting from the center. Serve 5 or 6 pieces, arranged in a circle, at one side of a cold dinner plate.
2. Next to pineapple at the right side, place 2 sections of grapefruit. Next to grapefruit, place 2 slices of orange, one overlapping the other. And next to oranges, place 2 cooked prunes on a half slice of lemon.
3. In center of plate, place 3 Tbsp. confectionery sugar . Next to sugar and partly covering it, pile 5 large, unhulled strawberries.
4. At left side of plate, between strawberries and pineapple, place ½ of a banana sliced all the way through, but still retaining its shape.

SERVES ONE (or perhaps a group to nibble for dessert).

Another take on ladies who lunch appears in a story, mysteriously printed as Lonesome Train. A newcomer to New York named Connie is being shown the sights on Fifth Avenue by an oldtimer, Miss Boland. After praying at

St. Patrick's Cathedral, Miss Boland says, "We'll all go to Schrafft's together . . . you'll like Schrafft's." Here is part of the charming episode that follows: Elderly ladies arriving for early lunch at Schrafft's seated themselves courteously, and removed their white gloves. The waitresses seemed to know some of them by name.

"Mrs. Andrews," a waitress placed a glass of sherry before one of the ladies nearby, "our specialty today is chicken à la king, would you like to try that?"

"No, Carrie, I'll have a cucumber sandwich with the crusts removed."

Another woman says she'll have the specialty of the day with a glass of sherry and yet another woman seconds that order.

Connie listened in to the nearby table talk, observing the gentility of the diners. She was intrigued because she knew of no Schrafft's-type place near her hometown. Unlike these women, most of the elderly ladies back home only went out to lunch when invited on some special occasion like Mother's Day.

The Connie in that story may have been impressed by the good manners of the women, but Susan Dodson got a good laugh out of their behavior. When she lunched with a friend at a Schrafft's counter in the City Hall area where she worked, she committed the crime of reaching in her purse to extract a lipstick. A well-dressed matron nearby stood up, stared at Susan, and said "Aren't you ashamed of yourself? Were you raised in a barn? Tch, tch, very bad manners!"

But whatever their manners or their finances, Big City folk always loved going to Schrafft's. Whether they were in a group or all alone, legions of ladies (and men as well) gravitated to these eateries and looked upon them as family establishments. In fact, one elderly widow left a note at her bedside saying, "*In case of death notify Schrafft's.*"

Worth remembering—and perhaps shedding a tear over—were those solitary diners, usually low-income ladies who came to Schrafft's for a frugal meal. W. H. Auden described one such woman "of indeterminate age" in his poem titled "In Schrafft's" which was later set to music in a choral work by Richard Edward Wilson.

As to those virtuous waitresses, their Irish eyes were often smiling for another reason. According to Frank McCourt in *Tis: A Memoir,* Schrafft's waitresses were famous for saving up to go home and buy the old family farm. Another one who was saving to go back to Ireland is described in awe as being a head waitress in Schrafft's and having her own apartment. McCourt added,

"They're hopeless in the city the way they all work at fancy places like Schrafft's" saying "Ah, yes, ma'am . . . indeed, ma'am, are the mashed potatoes a little too lumpy, ma'am?"

Here is an appropriate Schrafft's recipe in memory of those Irish women. . .

CORNED BEEF AND CABBAGE
WITH BOILED POTATO

(1961)

1. Cover 3 lbs corned beef with water. Bring to a boil, then turn down heat and simmer until tender, 2½ to 3 hours. Keep in water in which it was cooked.
2. Cut medium-size head of cabbage in wedges about 3 inches at widest part.
3. Plunge cabbage into a separate pot of boiling, salted water, cover, and cook until tender, 5 to 10 minutes. (Save small amount of cabbage stock to use if reheating cabbage later.)
4. Cut corned beef into 2 oz. slices. Serve 2 slices on one side of hot dinner plate. Next to meat, place a wedge of cabbage and medium-sized boiled potato.

"The Joint is Jumping!"

IF YOU THINK the atmosphere at Schrafft's was always tranquil, think again. After five o'clock at some locations, the bar scene really came alive. The drink list was extensive and put to constant use, causing a great deal of eccentric behavior despite Schrafft's reputation for proper decorum. According to a story in the *Saturday Evening Post,* a woman at the bar in the Times Square store suddenly did a ballet dance and departed turning cartwheels. Amidst the cocktail-lounge crowd at Rockefeller Center, another woman opened a Schrafft's cake box and a bluebird flew out, which she ran around the place to capture. And then there is the possibly apocryphal tale of a couple having trouble making love. Their doctor tells them to do

Bartenders as nattily dressed as their customers were kept busy at cocktail hour.

WHEN EVERYBODY ATE AT SCHRAFFT'S

it anywhere when the spirit seizes them. They report back to their doctor that his advice really worked, but they're not welcome at the bar in their neighborhood Schrafft's anymore.

Considering the care Schrafft's took in their choice of ingredients, it should come as no surprise that they were equally picky about the alcoholic beverages they purchased. They put spirits to the test just as they did food. A highly respected beverage salesman would meet with a special Schrafft's tasting panel to make the decision on what to buy based on quality and taste.

How drink prices and proportions have changed!

SCHRAFFT'S EXTRA-DRY MARTINI 95¢
(1967)

⅓ oz. French Vermouth
1⅔ oz. Gin

1. Stir in shaker glass with ice.
2. Strain with spoon strainer into a chilled cocktail glass.
3. Add an olive (or a small white onion to make it a Gibson Cocktail).

SCHRAFFT'S MANHATTAN COCKTAIL

approx. 90¢ (1965)

⅔ oz. Italian Vermouth★
1⅓ oz. Bar Rye

1. Stir with ice.
2. Strain with spoon strainer into cocktail glass.
3. Add cherry.

★One can assume that was sweet and not dry vermouth. The sweetness was deceptive, e.g. one woman remembers getting smashed on such seemingly innocent Schrafft's Manhattans and never touching the stuff again.

In 1968, a whole bottle of bubbly was offered for $6.50. Whiskey and cocktails ranged in price from 60¢ (Horse's Neck) to $1.75 (Mint Julep) with an average price around $1.00. A note in 1968 states: "Cocktails made with other than bar whiskies, charge .05 additional over the brand price." Among the cocktails popular at the time: Leap Year, Royal Smile, Scarlett O'Hara, Bloodhound, Bronx, Affinity, Presidential, Planters and Singapore Cocktails, and many others that sound more like names for racehorses than for drinks. Of course, there was the Pink Lady made with grenadine, whites of eggs, and gin, and for little girls, the nonalcoholic Shirley Temple with grenadine and ginger ale instead of gin. (In the dining rooms as well, children might have had ice cream sodas while Mommy sipped a Scotch-and-soda.)

Hot hors d'oeuvres were often served in the cocktail lounges and offered for catering. Here are two of the recipes that make enough for big parties.

⌘

MINIATURE MEATBALLS

(1960)

3 lbs. bottom round, chopped
3 Tbsp. onion juice
1 Tbsp. Worcestershire sauce
1½ tsp. salt
¼ tsp. pepper
1 cup finely ground, dried bread crumbs
1 cup canned beef gravy
olive oil (Crisco was used in original recipe)

1. Mix all but the last three ingredients together. Roll into tiny balls and then roll each ball in bread crumbs.
2. Cover bottom of a big skillet with oil. Cook meatballs in skillet, turning occasionally until brown on all sides. Transfer to a saucepan when cooked.

3. At party time, add the beef gravy and simmer until piping hot.

MAKES OVER 100 MINIATURE MEATBALLS.

CHEESE PUFFS

(1940; rewritten 1963)

3 egg whites
1½ cups cheddar cheese
1 Tbsp. flour
¼ tsp. salt
⅛ tsp. pepper
¼ tsp. mustard
½ tsp. Worcestershire sauce
1 cup finely ground, dried bread crumbs
oil for deep-frying

1. Mix first seven ingredients together and let stand in refrigerator before proceeding.
2. Scoop out puffs with small-size potato baller. Roll in bread crumbs.
3. Deep-fry to a golden brown in enough oil to cover. Serve on toothpicks.

MAKES APPROXIMATELY 50.

JAZZ AT NOON

IN A MANHATTAN club below the Schrafft's on East 58th Street, the joint really was jumping every Friday at lunchtime. Under the leadership of Les Lieber (who still conducts Jazz at Noon, now at Cafe St. Bart's in New York), professional people who were nonprofessional musicians would come to jam. Doctors, lawyers, dentists, architects, ad executives, and even CEO's would all have a ball, performing before an enthusiastic audience. Lieber remembers rewarding himself with a Schrafft's chocolate ice cream soda or chocolate malted after the gigs. "I'm doubly glad Jazz at Noon played near that oasis of chocolate," he recently remarked. As to what others may have been drinking there, it's safe to say, little work got done when they later returned to their offices.

As described in *On the Town in New York,* the Schrafft's at 21 West 51st Street ran all the way across to West 52nd Street where it faced The '21' Club. The two organizations were quite chummy and sometimes entertained each other. Schrafft's gave a party for the people working at '21' and they, in turn, celebrated Mrs. Shattuck's birthday. "Someone cried 'throw the cake over your shoulder for good luck,' and she did, and everyone laughed and laughed . . ."

Private groups also took advantage of the stores that had the most spacious interiors, staging parties there, catered by Schrafft's. At such events the fun-and-games involved could get out of hand. During one such affair, an advertising agency's party, an attractive Schrafft's waitress had to climb over barrels of dishes to escape the amorous clutches of an account executive.

That unruly guest couldn't possibly have been a Schrafft's regular, but one time, far worse happened to break the peace. In 1951 at the 77th Street and Madison Avenue store, a man dining with his wife and another fellow actually committed murder. He shot his wife to death and wounded the other guy, right at the table, before heading home to kill himself. As reported in the *Saturday Evening Post,* a newsman covering the shooting commented with dry humor that the setting "makes murder seem almost respectable." The murderer himself was apparently aware of the kind of place he was in because the waitress who served him and his unfortunate guests told the press, "He was a perfect gentleman. He paid his check first."

The dining room at the 77th Street and Madison Avenue store, back to normal after murder was committed here.

WHEN EVERYBODY ATE AT SCHRAFFT'S

The Fountain of Youth

IT'S IMPOSSIBLE TO think about Schrafft's without recalling the effect of the soda fountain treats on children. In *Tender at the Bone* (New York: Random House), *Gourmet Magazine* editor-in-chief, Ruth Reichl, describes the joy in her childhood of having her aunt say, "Let's go to Schrafft's!" adding that everyone envied her for it. One can picture the little girl's pleasure, slowly eating her chocolate-marshmallow sundae while "watching the women ascend the restaurant's wide, dramatic stairway."

Kids' memories of Schrafft's indulgences appear in countless books. One book reports that when she was a girl, Jacqueline Kennedy Onassis regularly lunched at Schrafft's with friends from school, particularly enjoying the pistachio ice cream. In

1185 Park Avenue: A Memoir Anne Rolphe tells about her mother taking her to Schrafft's "where Irish waitresses in black uniforms with white aprons serve chocolate syrup-filled sodas and chicken sandwiches with the crusts cut off." Stephen Dixon in his *All Gone: 18 Short Stories* has a character named Joe who describes being allowed to pocket a few sugar packets and have an ice cream soda while sitting on a phone book to reach the straws.

Grandmothers, who enjoyed Schrafft's with or without their grandkids, indulged many a child in sweet treats there. A former New Englander, Susan Cocco, writes that she and her *nonna* would dress up and go into Boston to shop before winding up at Schrafft's. "We would ride the 'T' into town on the Orange line which snaked its way past an imposing clock tower ablaze with the red Schrafft's logo. It signaled that wonderful things lay in store for me in the world of Boston—the unequivocal love of my grandmother and the delight of sharing the sweet, frosty goodness of ice cream at Schrafft's with her. To this day, I find no dessert more satisfying than vanilla ice cream, covered with chocolate sauce, and served in a silvered cup a la Schrafft's."

*Illustration by
Ann Shirazi*

The structure with the giant clock tower, erected by Schrafft's in 1928, was the nation's largest candy factory, where the company made its name in boxed chocolates. Sprawled across 900,000 square feet, the factory housed 1,500 employees. Still standing and visible from I-93, the towering building has been turned into an office complex.

Carrie Levin, the restaurateur, chef, and co-author of *The Good Enough to Eat Breakfast Cookbook,* bakes a luscious coffee cake that she designed to remind her of one she had at Schrafft's when her grandmother would take her there. She would get all dressed up in a frilly pink dress for those special occasions. (A warning: this cake requires kneading, rising, rolling. If you can master the extremely long recipe, you will graduate from baking school with honors!)

ORANGE-APRICOT-PECAN COFFEE CAKE

Makes 1 ten-inch cake

Carrie recommends using a standing electric mixer with paddle attachment and a piping bag with a number 230 tip.

1 packet dry yeast
¼ cup warm water (110 degrees)
pinch sugar
3 cups all-purpose flour plus 2 Tbsp. for flouring
1 tsp. salt
2 Tbsp. sugar

½ tsp. baking soda
1 orange
¼ cup sour cream
½ cup plus 2 Tbsp. scalded milk
2 eggs (white of 1 reserved for icing)
3 Tbsp. butter plus 1 Tbsp. for greasing bowl
3 Tbsp. cream cheese
¾ cup toasted pecan halves
¾ cup slivered dried apricots
3 Tbsp. apricot or peach jam
1 to 1¼ cups confectioners' sugar

Put the yeast into the warm water with the pinch of sugar and let it sit for 5 to 7 minutes in a warm spot for the sponge.

1. At low speed combine in the mixer the 3 cups of flour, salt, sugar, and baking soda. Zest the orange and save the rest. Combine two-thirds of the zest with the sour cream and scalded milk. Whisk 1 whole egg and 1 yolk in a separate bowl.

2. Add the 3 tablespoons of butter and cream cheese in small pieces to the mixer and combine until mixture is crumbly. (As a general rule, stop the mixer and scrape down the sides before every addition.) Add the eggs and beat for a few seconds. Add the milk mixture and beat a few seconds. Now add the yeast sponge and beat until the dough comes up around

the paddle and takes on a silky appearance.

3. Remove to the board. Flour the board only if the dough sticks. Knead a few times and place in a large glass bowl greased with the 1 tablespoon of butter.

4. Roll the dough to coat it, cover with a clean dish towel, and place in a warm spot to rise for 1 to 1-½ hours, until doubled.

5. The apricots should be put into enough boiling water to cover, with a slice of the zested orange. Let the water return to a boil, then turn off heat and let pot sit, covered, for 10 minutes. Drain water and pat apricots dry. Both apricots and the toasted pecan should be cool before using.

6. Bring the dough back to the board and cut it in half. Roll each piece into a rectangle approximately 4 x 12 inches. Reserve ¼ cup of the pecans and distribute the rest along with the apricots over the surface of your two rectangles of dough. Roll closed along the long side as tightly as you can without tearing the dough and pinch the long edge of the "snakes" into the dough surface to close.

(This last bit and what follows will test your mettle—you do not want to tear the dough. If you do, you won't receive your master's degree.)

7. Now roll the two snakes very carefully until they are about 18 inches long. Pinch the ends together.

Twine the snakes together—think herpetological love—and then form a ring about 8 inches across. (If you've gotten this far without mishap, I would discard the measuring tape.) Pinch the ends together, cover the ring, and let it rise for another ½ hour.

8. Preheat oven to 350°. You might want to do this earlier if the temperature in the kitchen is below 65 degrees, to help the dough rise.

For the glaze: Squeeze the juice from the zested orange and combine 1 tablespoon of the juice with 3 tablespoons apricot jam in a small pot. Simmer and stir until melted and mixed—about 10 minutes.

Back to the dough: Place the risen ring on a nonstick sheet or on parchment paper on a cookie sheet. Brush on the apricot glaze lavishly. Bake for 30 to 35 minutes, until golden brown. It should have a slightly hollow sound when tapped. Let it cool for 15 to 20 minutes before icing.

For the icing: Combine 2 tablespoons of egg white with the remaining third of orange zest, 1 tablespoon of the orange juice, and a generous cup of sifted confectioners sugar. Mix well until thick enough to put in the piping bag. Arrange the rest of the pecans on top of the cake, and apply the icing as though you were Jackson Pollack. That's it. Did you graduate? (Editor's note: If it sounds like too much work, enjoy similar treats at Good Enough To Eat.)

As to more youthful memories of Schrafft's, the author's son, Peter, says he distinctly remembers the cookies and candy up front that enticed kids (and their adult relatives). In fact, a woman named Grace Hechinger swears that her son Paul was a Schrafft's aficiando at the tender age of two, able to spot the name anywhere in town even before he saw the goodies inside or in the window. But a sweet tooth wasn't everything. Writing about his childhood visits to a suburban Schrafft's, a man mentions how the waitress there acted motherly to kids, and then he segues into a description of how much he liked the mashed potatoes served with lots of gravy. Like a real restaurant reviewer, he comments on the fact that "you could see the specks of pepper . . . which gave the potatoes a sharp, pointed taste that somehow went with the importance of the people there."

Dining area on the patio at Schrafft's in Eastchester, NY.

Indoors, a cook working at the charcoal barbecue grill.

For young and old alike, here is . . .

SCHRAFFT'S SPECIAL SAUCE
FOR BARBECUED CHICKEN

(1961) In a quantity to get any household through the
grilling entertainment season.
(Feel free to cut the recipe down to a smaller size.)

1 cup salad oil
2 lbs. finely chopped onion
1½ oz. garlic, finely minced
3 qts. water
3 cups lemon juice
1½ tsp. Tabasco sauce
9 oz. Worcestershire sauce
1½ qts. tomato catsup
1 Tbsp. dried oregano
3 Tbsp. chili powder
¾ cup granulated sugar
3 Tbsp. salt
1½ tsp. pepper

Heat oil, add onions and garlic, and sauté until trans-
parent. Add balance of ingredients, cover, and simmer
slowly for 15 minutes. Yield: 5 quarts

Naturally, the soda fountain hamburgers, cheeseburgers, hotdogs, and ice cream dishes were always big hits. And you couldn't go wrong offering a kid (or apparently George W. Bush) a simple little peanut butter sandwich...

PEANUT BUTTER WITH CURRANT JELLY
(1952)

Spread peanut butter evenly to edges of bottom slice of bread. Butter (yes, butter) the inside of top slice of bread and spread a spoonful of currant jelly to the edges. Place together, cut in half or thirds, and cut off the crusts.

(Schrafft's also offered peanut butter sandwiches with slices of BANANA or strips of crisp BACON for more sophisticated children—and peanut butter laced with CHILI SAUCE for the daring.)

However, one story goes to show that you can't please all of the kids all of the time. Virginia Borland reports that she took her five-year-old godchild, Brack Hazan, to the Schrafft's at 57th Street and Lexington Avenue. He got along famously with the Irish waitress, named Bridie, gobbled up all of his lunch and listened patiently when the dessert menu was read to him. Trouble arose when this otherwise angelic child demanded "ice cream with a handle on it." He cried and cried when nobody knew what he meant. Finally, when Virginia and he left Schrafft's and saw a Good Humor truck, the mystery was solved. He wanted one of *those* ice creams ... on a stick!

The Fans and the Pans

MOST CUSTOMERS PRAISED Schrafft's for offering a clean, comfortable, and congenial place to dine on tasty dishes, while some others (as in a Broadway show) took potshots at the food.

The height of respectability if not haute cuisine, the "stores" were a daily addiction of many people who took most of their meals there. In the famous tale, "The Catbird Seat," by James Thurber, the protagonist, Mr. Martin, has dinner at eight o'clock every night at the Schrafft's on Fifth Avenue near 46th Street, finishing his dinner and the financial page of the *Sun* at a quarter to nine. (Reading while eating was a common practice. One person reports that while his mother worked at Schrafft's she never

bought a newspaper because customers always left their copies behind.)

In recent years, an art history professor bemoaned the fact that "there was a time when the monolithic concrete slab that covers the Philippine consulate, on Fifth Avenue at 46th Street, was the neoclassical facade of a Schrafft's restaurant." Agreeing with that statement, *The AIA Guide to New York City* observes that "Its facade was cosmetized via radical plastic surgery into the Philippine Center." The guidebook does, however, speak kindly about a restaurant, now gone, that opened next door to the Center. A need for it was seen because "after the demise of the Brass Rail and Schrafft's, it was difficult to find a dignified but reasonably priced Fifth Avenue eatery."

Schrafft's first large restaurant in New York City was opened in 1919 at 48 Broad Street. Catering to the Wall Street crowd, Schrafft's sought to throw off the tearoom image there with heartier fare. Later, during the Depression, the stores acted like life rafts, helping suddenly impoverished people stay afloat by offering meals in pleasant surroundings for very little. Even during the food shortages in World War II, the stores continued to flourish. (To cope with the scarcity of sugar during wartime, sweeteners such as honey often found their way into the baked goods.) But the best was yet to be. After the war, Schrafft's growth was phenomenal. During the boom period in 1948 E. B. White wrote in *Here Is New York*, "Money has been plentiful and New York has responded. Restaurants are hard to get into; businessmen stand in line for a Schrafft's luncheon as meekly as idle men used to stand in soup lines . . . The lunch hour in Manhattan has been shoved ahead half an hour, to 12:00 or 12:30, in the hopes of beating the crowd to a table." Similarly, an article by Babbette Brandt Fromme in *Avenue* states that in the Men's Grill at 48 Broad Street, "The line [of people waiting for tables] often went right up the stairs." To encourage the impatient crowd, the manager marked each step with the waiting time . . . And he would promise to buy lunch for anyone not seated within the stated time."

The bar at the Men's Grill on Broad Street before the crowd of customers descended upon it.

Along with hearty steaks, roasts, and chops, here is a lunchtime sandwich specially designed for the Men's Grill:

SARDINE, SPANISH ONION AND TOMATO OPEN RYE BREAD SANDWICH

(1956)

1. Butter 2 slices of sandwich rye to the edges. Cover one slice with 4 sardines, split lengthwise and placed horizontally, round side up.
2. On other slice of bread, place 2 slices of Spanish onion, cut thin. Top the onion with 3 slices of ¼-inch thick tomato.
3. Serve open on a 12-inch platter garnished with a sprig of watercress.
4. Next to sardines, place a lemon wedge along with some tartar sauce in a small lettuce cup. Next to the onion/tomato bread slice, place a few potato chips.

TOKENS OF AFFECTION

IN STORE AFTER store, customers became so attached to the help, they rewarded favorite waitresses with valuable gifts from stock shares to mink coats and often remembered them in their wills. And the same goes for male employees. In fact,

WHEN EVERYBODY ATE AT SCHRAFFT'S

one popular soda jerk inherited thousands of dollars from a regular at his counter. One waitress not only received furs, but the hand in marriage of the rich furrier who bestowed the gift. Another, working at the financial district Schrafft's, became such a pal of a broker and his wife, she was invited to spend all her weekends at the couple's country estate.

SCHRAFFT'S AND SHOW BIZ

IN THE FILM *The Solid Gold Cadillac,* a scene is set in the spiffy Rockefeller Center store. Here, Judy Holliday and Paul Douglas bump into each other, then sit and talk before leaving together.

In the Broadway version of Neil Simon's *Barefoot in the Park*, the young husband makes an appointment to meet his law partner in Schrafft's at 8 A.M. to go over briefs. The name pops up again in Simon's *The Odd Couple* when Oscar says, "You want to play poker, deal the cards. You want to eat, go to Schrafft's." In a sense, you could say that Schrafft's was ahead of its time. Long before nouvelle cuisine, Schrafft's had a reputation for serving dainty portions, a la their tearoom past. (In 1923 a Schrafft's Tea-room Orchestra played on radio station WJZ, New York.) This belief that the servings tended to be rather small led a character in the Broadway production of *Seven Year Itch* to deliver the joke line, "I'm hungry. I just had dinner at Schrafft's." And then there was the scene in Billy Wilder's film, *The Apartment*. When Baxter asks his neighbor, Dr. Dreyfuss, if he had a late call, the doctor says "Yeah.

Some clown at Schrafft's 57th Street ate a club sandwich and forgot to take out the toothpick."

But in her inimitable style, the poet Phyllis McGinley had the last word on the restaurants' fame: "Yes, dear to my heart as to Midas his coffers / Are the noontime tables at Schrafft's and Stouffer's." Hmm, Stouffer's was obviously in there just for the sake of the rhyme!

On the other hand, there were those who considered Schrafft's too straight-laced and stuffy while some considered the stores' way of doing things downright laughable. Worse, the Broadway revue, *Make Mine Manhattan,* that opened in 1948, later gave birth to a zany song called "Schrafft's" that needled the place unmercifully—and unjustly. Apparently left out of the original production, in 1977 the song resurfaced in one of Ben Bagley's Great Revues Revisited. In it, lyricist Arnold B. Horwitt not only laughed at the Schrafft's staff, but lobbed a grenade at the place with bizarre food descriptions, ending the song with a zinger about the so-called small portions.

Cover of the CD which includes the infamous song, "Schrafft's," as sung by Helen Gallagher.

In Schrafft's there is a tingle in the name,
Schrafft's where all the dishes taste the same.
Your heart will sing, your soul will feel exalted
Ordering a double frosted chocolate malted.
Schrafft's, where you can eat right off the floor,
Schrafft's, and you'll enjoy it even more.
The spoons are clean, there's magic in the Ovaltine
In Schrafft's, Schrafft's, Schrafft's.
There's a hostess to greet you
And a hostess to seat you
And a hostess who's giving commands.
There's a girl who brings the water
And a girl who takes your order
And a girl who don't do nuthin, she just stands.

Then comes a moment when you feel gay as any bride
You open up the menu and God almighty the things inside
Asparagus tips with butterscotch syrup surrounded by sardines
Hard-boiled eggs with maraschino cherries in monogrammed terrines
Cream of wheat with pistachio nuts
Chili con carne with marshmallow sauce
Then for dessert, a mocha coconut deep dish custard pie
With Russian dressing of course.

Schrafft's, where all the help are so well-bred
Schrafft's, you should be serving them instead.
You can eat all night, it won't affect your appetite
In Schrafft's, Schrafft's, Schrafft's.

Breakfast at Schrafft's

(THE TIFFANY OF MORNING DINING SPOTS)

OFTEN AS POPULAR first thing in the day as late at night, Schrafft's had its breakfast regulars. In *Citizen Newhouse* by Carol Feisenthal, we learn that the media giant Samuel Newhouse often ate breakfast alone at the counter of Schrafft's. Similarly infatuated, a man named Isaac Newton Phelps Stokes had kind words to say about starting out the day at Schrafft's. A former millionaire who lost his shirt in the Depression, Stokes still managed to dine regularly at Schrafft's and called the 40¢ breakfast "a marvel of civilization." And in a memoir about growing up in the Bronx, Azar Attura lauds the "leisurely and wonderful breakfasts at Schrafft's."

While the phrase "power breakfast" had not been coined as yet, many movers and shakers did congregate at

Schrafft's as they do today in the restaurant at New York's Regency Hotel, making deals over egg dishes that didn't cost anything like the Regency's $17 omelet.

Nutrition guru Adelle Davis advised, "Eat breakast like a king, lunch like a prince, and dinner like a pauper," and many Schrafft's customers followed that suggestion. The morning choices at Schrafft's were the greatest in their time and went from the simple to the fanciful. Among the regal possibilities were rich dishes like Cinnamon Apple, Blueberry, and Pecan Pancakes using a griddle cake mix, and very filling specialties like Creamed Codfish and Creamed Finnan Haddie dating back to 1928-29, served with fried potatoes. But let's go a little lighter on the dishes that might have been within Stokes's early-morning budget with several easygoing recipes.

BANANA OMELET WITH BACON CURLS
(1930)

1. Peel a banana, cut into ¼-inch slices, and sprinkle with 1 tsp. lemon juice.
2. Sauté ⅓ of the banana (8 slices) in 1 Tbsp. butter until very light brown.
3. Lightly whisk 2 eggs, cook in 1 Tbsp. butter to make omelets, and just before folding, add the sautéed banana.

4. Bacon curls are made by rolling up slices of raw bacon, placing them on a rack in a pan, and baking in oven until crisp. Serve 1 curl on each side of omelet.

CHICKEN LIVER SAUTÉ ON TOAST

(1927; rewritten 1960)

1. Dredge 2 large or 3 small, raw chicken livers in flour seasoned with salt and pepper. Sauté in 1 Tbsp. butter (old recipe used chicken fat).
2. Remove livers and add a little hot water to pan to make a gravy with the butter.
3. Place a slice of buttered toast, cut in half diagonally, on a hot plate. Pour gravy over toast and place livers on top.
4. Position 2 strips of freshly cooked, crisp bacon crosswise over the chicken livers.

SCRAMBLED EGGS COUNTRY STYLE
SERVED WITH COOKED TOMATOES
(1925-1926)

QUANTITY RECIPE FOR THE TOMATOES:
1¾ cups canned tomatoes
5 tsp. flour
2 tsp. sugar
½ tsp. salt
4 Tbsp. butter
¼ tsp. pepper
1 scant Tbsp. onion, chopped

1. Cook tomatoes and sugar together for 3 minutes.
2. In another pan, melt butter and sauté onions in it. Add and cook the flour.
3. Add flour and onion mixture to the tomatoes. Cook until tomatoes are slightly thickened. Offer a small portion with the eggs, saving the rest for other uses.

SCRAMBLED EGGS COUNTRY STYLE—SERVING ONE:
1. Heat omelet pan. Add and melt 1 tsp. butter in it.
2. Drop in 2 *unbeaten* eggs. When they begin to set, beat slightly with a fork—just enough to scramble the eggs a little.
3. Do not cook until eggs are dry. They should be set, but cooked soft.

Celebrity Hangouts

PATRICIA NEAL PROUDLY reports that the great playwright Eugene O'Neill sipped chocolate sodas with her at Schrafft's. Broadway star, Marian Seldes says "I LOVED Schrafft's," fondly recalling the black-and-white sodas, and Eli Wallach remembers dining at Schrafft's near the theatre where he was in rehearsal for a play. In a television rebroadcast about Steve Allen, his wife, Jayne Meadows, related how on first meeting her, Allen, who was very shy, summoned up his courage to say, "Let's go over to Schrafft's and have dessert." Helen Gallagher, who sang the snide song about Schrafft's in *Make Mine Manhattan,* is another person who tells a nice story about how much her grandmother loved Schrafft's, often taking her there before a matinee.

But the best story is about a young actor named Kirk Douglas who was as yet undiscovered when he waited tables uptown at Schrafft's 2285 Broadway store, where a Barnes & Noble Superstore is located now. In a 1954 article by Bob Thomas, Douglas tells how he took the job at Schrafft's when he had only 20¢ to his name and couldn't afford to buy a meal. Claiming that the waiters on his shift weren't allowed to eat, he committed what was the one cardinal sin among Schrafft's employees: *he stole food.* He also figured out a way to earn more tips. He would speed up the turnover by hovering around the tables he served so that customers would get the message and leave more quickly.

Douglas had two regular customers who were friends of his from the American Academy of Dramatic Arts. One was Diana Dill, whom he later married. The other was Betty Joan Perske, better known as Lauren Bacall.

WHEN EVERYBODY ATE AT SCHRAFFT'S

The Broadway at 82nd St. location where Kirk Douglas once worked, and where books are now sold instead of meals.

STAR-GAZING MADE EASY

STAR-STRUCK CUSTOMERS could seek their prey in any number of Schrafft's locations, ranging from cozy, neighborhood places to the elegant store in the Chrysler Building to the hugely glamorous, four-level affair in the ESSO Building at Rockefeller Center where many celebrities were regulars. *(See Chapter 15 for photographs and details.)* Among the famous folk spotted at various Schrafft's were singers like Kate Smith, actors like Richard Kiley, Ingrid Bergman, Janet Leigh, Myrna Loy, and Margaret Sullivan; and political figures such as President Harry Truman and his daughter Margaret, First Lady Pat Nixon, and New York Mayor Robert Wagner. Bandleader Guy Lombardo, dance impressario Arthur Murray, and Admiral Hyman Rickover might have bumped into each other at the Schrafft's stores they frequented. Marilyn Monroe and Arthur Miller were seen dining together. And didn't you spot Bennett Cerf and Arlene Francis discussing "What's My Line" at the corner table?

After naming names of V.I.P.s who really did go to Schrafft's, here's a fictional look at the subject. A hilarious spoof by S.J. Perelman makes the celebrity chase at the stores his target in a 1941 story.

WHEN EVERYBODY ATE AT SCHRAFFT'S

A Pox On You, Mine Goodly Host

BY S.J. PERELMAN

A FEW NIGHTS ago I strolled into our Pompeian living room in my stocking feet, bedad, with a cigar in my mouth and a silk hat tilted back on my head, to find Maggie, with osprey plumes in her hair and a new evening cape, pulling on long white gloves. A little cluster of exclamation points and planets formed over her head as she saw me.

"Aren't you dressed yet, you bonehead?" she thundered. "Or were you sneaking down to Dinty Moore's for corned beef and cabbage with those worthless cronies of yours?" I soon banished the good woman's fears, and in response to my queries she drew from her reticule an advertisement clipped from the *Sun*. It displayed photographs of George S. Kaufman and Moss Hart framed in a family album over the legend "From Schrafft's Album of Distinguished Guests. The parade of luminaries who enjoy Schrafft's hearty dinners includes columnists, sports writers, stage and radio personalities, football coaches, illustrators, producers. Adding to the glitter of this list are the distinguished names of Kaufman and Hart, who have written many a Broadway hit." Of course, nothing would do but we must dine at Schrafft's that very evening and mingle in the pageantry, so without further ado we set out.

Although it was not yet seven o'clock when our cab pulled up in front of the Forty-third Street branch, a sizable crowd of autograph-seekers had assembled and were eagerly scrutinizing each new arrival. A rapturous shout went up as I descended. "Here comes dashing Brian Aherne!" exulted a charming miss rushing forward. "Isn't it sickening?" I murmured into my wife's ear. "This happens everywhere—in stores, on buses—" "Yes, I know," she grated. "Everybody takes me for Olivia de Havilland. Get out of the way, you donkey. Don't you see the man's trying to get by?" To my surprise, I found myself brushed aside by Brian Aherne, who must have been clinging to the trunk rack. As I shouldered my way after him, curious stares followed me. "That must be his bodyguard," commented a fan. "That shrimp couldn't be a cat's bodyguard," sneered his neighbor. I looked the speaker full in the eye. "That's for the cat to say," I riposted, and as the bystanders roared, I stalked through the revolving doors, conscious I had scored.

Buoyant the advertisement had been, but I was frankly dazzled by the scene which confronted me. The foyer, ablaze with lights, was peopled by personages of such distinction as few first nights attract. Diamonds of the finest water gleamed at the throats of women whose beauty put the gems to shame, and if each was not escorted by a veritable Adonis, was at least a Greek. A hum of well-bred conversation rose from the throng, punctuated now and again by the click of expensive dentures. In one corner Nick Kenny, Jack Benny, James Rennie, Sonja Henie, and E. R. Penney, the chain-store magnate, were gaily comparing pocketbooks to see who had the most money, and in another Jim Thorpe chatted with Jay Thorpe, cheek and jowl with Walter Wanger and Percy Grainger. Here Lou Little and Elmer Layden demonstrated a new shift to a fascinated circle, while Ann Corio demonstrated still another to an even more spellbound circle. Myron Selznick, Frank Orsatti, and Leland Hayward had just planed in from the Coast to sign everyone to agency contracts, and now, swept along by sheer momentum, were busily signing each other. As far as the eye could see, at tables in the background, gourmets were gorging themselves on chicken-giblet-and-cream-cheese sandwiches, apple pandowdy, and orange snow. One fine old epicure, who had ordered a sizzling platter without specifying what food was to be in it, was nevertheless eating the platter itself and smacking his lips noisily. Small wonder that several world-famed illustrators, among them Henry Raleigh, Norman Rockwell and Pruett Carter, had set up easels and were limning the brilliant scene with swift strokes. I was drinking in every detail of the shifting panorama when a hostess well over nine feet tall, with ice mantling her summit, waved me toward a door marked "Credentials."

"We—we just wanted the old-fashioned nut pudding with ice-cream sauce, Ma'am," I stammered.

"That's up to the committee, Moozer," she said briskly, "If we let in every Tom, Dick and Harry who wanted the old-fashioned nut pudding with ice-cream sauce . . . Ah, good evening, Contessa! Back from Hobe Sound already?"

I entered a small room exquisitely furnished in Biedermeier and took my place in a short queue of applicants. Most of them were obviously under tension, and the poor wretch in front of me was a pitable spectacle. His eyes rolled wildly, tremors shook his frame, and it was apparent he entertained small hope of meeting the rigorous requirements.

"What have Kaufman and Hart got that I haven't got?" he demanded of me desperately. "I bought a house in Bucks County and wrote two plays, both smash hits, even if they didn't come to New York. Why, you ought to see the reviews *Tea and Strumpets* and *Once in a Wifetime* got in Syracuse!" I reassured him as best I could, but his premonitions were well founded, for a few moments later he was ignominiously dispatched to dine at a cafeteria. I was shuffling forward to confront the tight-lipped examiners when a scuffle broke out in the foyer and Kaufman and Hart, bundled in astrakhan greatcoats and their eyes flashing fire, were herded in unceremoniously.

"What is the meaning of this—this bestiality?" sputtered Hart. "How dare you bar us from this bourgeois *bistro?*"

"I've been thrown out of better restaurants than this!" boomed Kaufman, rapidly naming several high-class restaurants from which he had been ejected. The chairman of the board picked up a dossier and turned a cold smile on the playwrights.

"Naturally, we regret any inconvenience to you gentlemen," he said smoothly, "but our house rules are inflexible. You wrote a play called *Lady in the Dark,* did you not, Mr. Hart?" Hart regarded him stonily. "Starring Gertrude Lawrence, I believe?"

"Yes," snapped Hart, "and she's sitting right up at the fountain this minute having a rum-and-butter-toffee sundae with chopped pecans."

"Why were we not shown the script of that play, Mr. Hart?" The chairman's voice was silky with menace. "Why was nobody in the Frank G. Shattuck organization consulted regarding casting?"

"I—I meant to," quavered Hart. "I swear I did! I told my secretary—I made a note—"

"Thought you'd smuggle it into town without us, did you?" snarled the chairman. "Let 'em read the out-of-town notices in *Variety,* eh?" A tide of crimson welled up the alabaster column of Hart's neck, and he stood downcast, staring at his toecaps. Kaufman would fain have interceded for his associate, but the chairman stopped him with a curt gesture.

"Hamburg Heaven for thirty days," he barked. "Take 'em away."

"Help, help!" screamed the luckless duo, abasing themselves. But no vestige of pity lurked in the chairman's granite visage, and an instant later they were borne, kicking and squealing, from the chamber by two brawny attendants.

And now little else remains to be told. How I managed to elude my captors and steal the superb mocha cupcake the natives call "The Star of Forty-Third Street Between Sixth Avenue and Broadway" must be left to another chronicle.

Suffice to say that whenever your mother and I pass Schrafft's, she turns to me with a secret smile and we continue right on up to Lindy's. We can still get in there without a visa.

Proof that some of the truest things are said in jest, in *Capote: A Biography* by Gerald Clarke, Mary Louise, a good buddy of Truman Capote, shows that like Perelman's farcical people, Tru didn't fare too well in the stores. She said, "Truman was never embarrassed about speaking his mind, and we got thrown out of practically every Schrafft's in New York because we laughed so much."

The real Forty-third Street branch of S.J. Perelman's imaginary tale. Could that be some of his celebrities crowded into the dining area?

THE BAD NEWS: NOT EVERYONE WAS WELCOME

CAPOTE MAY HAVE been thrown out of Schrafft's, but sad to say, before the Civil Rights Act of 1964, there were people who barely got through the door. Segregation was rampant inside and outside Manhattan in hotels, banks, coffee shops, and restaurants, and Schrafft's was no exception. Brenda Dixon Gottschild touches on the topic in *Waltzing in the Dark: African American Vaudeville and Race Politics in the Swing Era*. She mentions that the famous African-American dancer Josephine Baker was denied a room in the St. Moritz Hotel while her Italian husband/manager and French maid were acceptable.

The situation was not much different in Harlem, of all places. True, in the 1920s and 1930s, there were cellars, lounges, cafes, rib joints, and countless bars and grills open to one and all, with illegal hooch during Prohibition. But just like places along the Great White Way, virtually all the Harlem theaters excluded blacks, including one where Fats Waller was playing the organ for the silent movies. Smalls' Paradise and the Savoy Ballroom welcomed both blacks and whites, but other nightspots like The Cotton Club and Connie's Inn were WHITES ONLY places, catering to the "swells" from downtown. New York mayor Jimmy Walker, stars like George Raft and Mae West, and even some Vanderbilts arrived in their limos. Ironically, all the performers were African Americans. The great Louis

WHEN EVERYBODY ATE AT SCHRAFFT'S

Armstrong's Orchestra played at Connie's. Owned by a notorious bootlegger who needed an outlet for his booze, the Cotton Club even turned away W.C. Handy despite having Duke Ellington and later Cab Calloway on the bandstand. The revues were legendary. Ethel Waters was one of the featured singers and "Lovely Tan Chorines" otherwise known as light-skinned, sepia "high-yaller" girls, stepped to tunes by important white songwriters.

Meanwhile, back at Schrafft's, according to Brenda Dixon Gottschild's book, "the staff waited on whites and ignored any blacks present. They didn't utter a racist word, but their message was clear." Whites waited on whites. Once, to brighten the spirit of diners during the Depression, Schrafft's hired a dance band to play at a store, but it didn't work out. Could it be because they didn't have rhythm? The good news is that some good souls, black and white, broke the color barrier. Lena Horne, who started her career as a 16-year-old chorine at the Cotton Club, didn't stay away from Schrafft's. On one occasion, she went to Schrafft's to have a cake decorated with musical symbols for her husband's birthday. And in Laurence Learner's *The Kennedy Women: The Saga of an American Family* he reports that "at a time when blacks rarely ventured below Harlem for social activities, Pat (Ethel Kennedy's sister) and a black student went to lunch together at Schrafft's in midtown Manhattan, effectively desegregating the popular restaurant.

13

"Comfort Food," Comfortably Priced

ARGUABLY THE TOP counter-and-tablecloth group of restaurants in the Northeast, Schrafft's offered a choice of dining diversions to celebs, neighborhood people, and tourists. You could munch a sandwich at the fountain, indulge in a full meal in the dining room, or just clink glasses and drink—all at modest cost in relaxing, eye-pleasing surroundings.

In all the stores, Schrafft's main dishes had a way of making people feel good. Here are recipes for some of this "comfort food."

MUSHROOM SAUCE A LA SCHRAFFT'S

(1936; rewritten 1957)

TO SERVE ON ANY KIND OF CHOPS
1 cup (½ lb.) unsalted butter—
instead of chicken fat in original recipe
¼ cup chopped onion
¼ cup chopped parsley
1 cup flour
5 cups chicken broth
2 cups mushrooms, sliced and sautéed
1 tsp. salt
juice of ½ lemon

1. Melt butter in saucepan. Add onion and parsley. When about half-cooked, add flour.
2. When well-blended, add chicken broth, mushrooms, salt and lemon.
3. Cover pan and let simmer for 20 minutes.

How to serve: Braise or broil chops. Place 2 (1 large, 1 small) at one side of hot dinner plate. Cover with Mushroom Sauce. Place a baked potato at the other side and a vegetable in a side dish.

VEAL CHOP SAUTÉ

(1942; rewritten 1963)

1. Preheat oven to 350°. Dredge chops with flour, salt, and pepper just before cooking.
2. Place ¼ cup butter and ¼ cup Crisco (or all butter?) in a large frying pan. Melt and then completely cover pan with chops, so that they almost overlap.
3. Let brown well on both sides, making sure butter does not burn. Place chops in an ovenproof pan.
4. Rinse out original frying pan with 1½ cups water and pour over chops. Place in oven.
5. As soon as chops are browned and glazed and some of the liquid has cooked away, add ½ cup more water. Cover and continue cooking until done—total time 30 minutes.

To serve: Place a chop on a hot dinner plate with a little of the pan gravy poured over it. Serve with 2 vegetables.

WELSH RAREBIT

(1959)

Sometimes jokingly called Welsh Rabbit, this cheese lover's delight required lots of toast to dip and dig into it.

6 Tbsp. butter
5 Tbsp. cornstarch
2 cups warmed light cream
1½ tsp. dry mustard, thoroughly dissolved in 4 tsp. cold water
5 tsp. Worcestershire sauce
dash of pepper
3 lbs. cheddar cheese, crumbled
½ cup warmed beer (Schrafft's used Budweiser)

1. Using top pot of a 2-qt. double boiler, melt butter, add cornstarch, and stir until very smooth with no lumps.
2. Add the warm cream and stir constantly with a spoon (not a wire whisk) so no lumps form. Then add the dissolved mustard.
3. The instant it starts to thicken, put the top pot on the bottom pot of the double boiler, where water must be boiling.
4. Beat rapidly with spoon so lumps disappear. Add Worcestershire sauce, pepper, and crumbled cheese.

5. Keep in double boiler in which the water does *not* boil. Beer flavor lasts over an hour, but if rarebit stands too long with beer in it, it will have a bitter taste.

How to serve: For each portion, place 1 ladle (4 oz.) of rarebit in bottom of a heated oval scallop dish. Put 2 diagonal pieces of toast on it. Press down so the rarebit comes up over the top of toast. Pour another 4 oz. ladle over it. Re-heat dish to bubble and when bubbling, place 4 triangles of toast across center of rarebit.

Put on platter with a dinner plate and serving spoon alongside it. Offer 2 extra slices of dry toast, cut diagonally, on a bread-and-butter plate.

YIELD: 6 SERVINGS OF RAREBIT

"COMFORT ME WITH APPLES"

IRISH-STYLE RINGS (1956)

A relish that people relished with pork or as a sweet snack

5 baking apples
¾ qt. of water
¾ cup granulated sugar
2 tsp. lemon juice

1. Preheat oven to 275°. Wash and core apples. Slice each apple crosswise in 3 rings.
2. Put the 15 rings in a pan. Add water and lemon juice, basting the rings with the liquid.
3. Sprinkle ¼ cup sugar over top of rings and place in oven. Bake until rings start to soften, approximately 10 minutes.
4. Remove from oven. Baste again and sprinkle with remaining sugar.
5. Place under broiler, basting until apples are cooked and lightly browned. .

SERVES 4 OR 5 AS A SIDE DISH.

LET'S TAKE A POWDER
TO BOSTON FOR CHOWDER
(AND BOSTON BAKED BEANS, OF COURSE)

WITH ITS NEW ENGLAND heritage, it figures that Schrafft's stores were good ports-of-call for seafood. Included on the list of soups were Cape Cod Clam Chowder, Boston Clam Chowder, Old Fashioned Clam Chowder, Seafood Chowder, and New England Fish Chowder, plus many other fishy dishes.

On a cold winter's day, it pays to make enough of lusty soup like this. So here's the recipe for *five quarts.*

OLD-FASHIONED CLAM CHOWDER
(1964)

2 lbs. chowder clams, chopped to about ⅜ inches each
5 cups clam liquid
5 cups canned tomatoes
1¼ cups diced carrots (¼-inch)
2 cups peeled, diced potatoes (¼-inch)
1 cup diced green peppers (¼-inch)
⅔ cup diced onions (¼-inch)
1 Tbsp. salt
⅓ tsp. pepper
⅔ Tbsp sugar
1⅔ qts. water
⅔ tsp. dried thyme

1. Strain the liquid that comes with the clams through double cheesecloth. Wash the raw clams in this liquid, picking over carefully to remove any pieces of shell.
2. Strain the clam liquid again through cheesecloth and add enough water to bring the amount up to the required 1¼ qts.
3. Add tomatoes, carrots, potatoes, green peppers, and onions to clam liquid and cook until the vegetables are soft.
4. Add chopped clams, salt, pepper, sugar, and water. Simmer slowly for 1½ hours. Stir in thyme after cooking. For each serving, ladle 6 oz. into a hot soup cup with saltine crackers on the side.

BOSTON BAKED BEANS
TO SERVE A SMALL ARMY

(1939; revised 1952)

Naturally, with Schrafft's background, the beans were unbeatable. They jazzed up servings of knackwurst or frankfurters—or did a solo act with a side dish of chili sauce and cole slaw. The more the merrier; here's how to make a large potful for a troop of people.

8 cups dry navy beans
2 tsp. club soda
1 lb. salt pork
1 cup chopped onions
1 cup brown sugar
1 cup molasses
3 Tbsp. salt
2 Tbsp. English mustard
1 tsp. pepper
1 tsp. ground ginger
1 tsp. paprika
½ cup flour
3½ qts. boiling water

1. Soak beans overnight. Next morning, cover with cold water and bring to a boil. Add soda and boil for a few minutes.

2. Rinse off soda water, place beans in large pot, and add salt pork and onions.
3. Thoroughly mix together all the other ingredients including the boiling water and pour over the beans.
4. Preheat oven to 350°. Cover pot and bake in the hot oven until reboiling. Then simmer gently for 6 hours, adding just enough boiling water when and if necessary to keep it from becoming dry.
5. Turn off the oven and let pot stand there overnight. Bake 2 hours the following day.

How to serve: Remove beans from pot. Add ½ cup catsup. Fill individual bean pots, placing a piece of pork on top of each. Brown in the oven.

WHEN EVERYBODY ATE AT SCHRAFFT'S

CRABMEAT AND NOODLES AU GRATIN

(1963)

It helps to have individual scallop dishes for this delicious recipe adapted from the original.

6 oz. butter
4 oz. flour
salt & pepper
6 cups milk, heated
3 Tbsp. lemon juice
2 Tbsp. chopped parsley
2 egg yolks
2 Tbsp. light cream
1½ pounds noodles, cooked and drained well
2 pounds fresh crabmeat in ¾-inch dice
⅔ cup grated cheddar cheese
¼ cup bread crumbs
paprika

1. Melt butter, add flour, salt & pepper, and cook until well blended, about 5 minutes. Then add hot milk gradually, stirring constantly until thickened and thoroughly cooked.
2. Add lemon juice and chopped parsley, blending well. Then add mixture of egg yolks and cream, bring to boil, and remove from heat.

3. Add cooked, drained noodles mixed with diced crabmeat.

How to serve:

- Place 2 scoops of mixture in each scallop dish. Sprinkle each with 1 Tbsp. grated cheddar, 1 tsp. bread crumbs, and a dash of paprika.
- Place under broiler to brown.
- Garnish end of dish with sprig of parsley. Place on tea plate. Offer extra plates with serving spoons.

YIELD: 8 TO 10 PORTIONS.

WHEN EVERYBODY ATE AT SCHRAFFT'S

COLD SENGALESE [*SIC*] SOUP

(1960)

Early in Schrafft's history it would have been surprising to find something so foreign-sounding on the menu. But the times they were a-changing and this slightly curried soup with its slightly misspelled African name was a refreshing change of pace on a hot American day.

2 Tbsp. finely diced onion
2 Tbsp. butter
2 tsp. curry powder
1 Tbsp. flour
3½ cups chicken broth
4 egg yolks, slightly beaten
2 cups light cream, chilled
¼ cup finely diced chicken breast meat
pinch of chopped parsley

1. Sauté onion in butter until soft, but not browned. Add curry powder and flour, cooking slowly for 5 minutes.
2. Add chicken broth and bring to boil, stirring until smooth. Then add egg yolks, stir and cook for 1 minute.
3. Put through fine mesh strainer and refrigerate until well-chilled. Then add the chilled cream and chicken.

How to serve: Very cold soup should be poured into un-handled cups set on saucers. Sprinkle with pinch of parsley. Yield: 6 portions

VEGETABLE DINNER,
ARTFULLY ARRANGED
(1939)

LONG BEFORE VEGETARIAN eating was in vogue, Schrafft's had a way of making such cuisine extremely attractive. Here's how . . .

- Put a scoop of mashed potatoes or a small, baked Idaho potato in the center of a dinner plate. Around that, put 5 vegetables in season.★
- Be very sure that the vegetables are well-cooked and hot, and that the plate looks neat.
- Do NOT put 2 vegetables of the same color next to one another on the plate.

Be sure to vary the colors.

- Combinations to use from time to time: buttered peas, carrots, spinach, celery hearts, and turnips or squash.

🍂 Other seasonal possibilities are lima beans, string beans, butter beans, beets, and onions.

★ Now, as you know, thanks to produce from other countries, almost every kind of vegetable is "in season" all year round.

CREAMED SHRIMP IN A PATTY SHELL
(1928; revised 1961)

People who say they liked the Chicken à la King surely must have *loved* the shrimp similarly cooked. Yum!

3 lbs. shrimp
1 cup butter
¼ cup lemon juice
1 tsp. paprika
½ grated onion

FOR THE SAUCE
¾ cup flour
1¼ qts. milk
¾ cup light cream
salt & pepper

1. Shell the shrimp and sauté in butter with lemon juice, paprika, and onion. Remove from pan and set aside.
2. Make sauce in the same butter, mixing the ingredients together, and then stirring and cooking on low heat for 5 minutes.
3. Strain sauce and add the shrimp.

How to serve: Ladle creamed shrimp into patty shells (or on rice) on dinner plates. Garnish with parsley.

YIELD: 8 OR 9 PORTIONS.

CASH & CAREY

FEW PEOPLE WHO patronized the stores were aware that Schrafft's ran executive dining rooms for more than 100 companies coast-to-coast and cafeterias serving thousands. Schrafft's employees also poured some 30 million cups of coffee a year from wagons wheeled into office buildings.

Trying to raise some cash for a trip to Ireland when she was 17, author Alice Carey worked as a summer replacement in several of the corporate dining rooms—moving around from Seagram's to Citicorp to a downtown New York insurance company. The rules were strict: (1) Long hair to be pinned up in a bun and tucked into a hairnet. (2) No on-the-job eating. (3) No tips.

According to Carey, old waitresses in semi-retirement seemed to have been moved to these dining rooms, perhaps because the hours were shorter, just 11 A.M. to 3 P.M. One wonders whether the age of these women was the reason they were issued *grey* uniforms instead of the black ones used in the stores.

Being the youngest and greenest, Carey got much of the dirty-work, cleaning up after the others, though she also served. With the men in

Alice Carey carries a tray à la Schrafft's.

Photograph by Eric Slomanson

the scullery constantly flirting with her, carrying the tray of food on one arm, Schrafft's style, from kitchen to table was to her a scary experience. So much so, the dish she once was trying to serve slid down the tray. Not wanting to clean up the floor if the dish ended up there, she put her elbow into the hot food to stop its journey, burning herself and, heaven help her, soiling her uniform.

Lesson learned, Alice Carey stretched out her arm one day recently to demonstrate and said, "I can still do The Tray!"

Here's another of the special dishes made from Schrafft's leftover roasts that delighted all those businessmen—when it made it safely to their tables.

PAN-BROWNED ROAST BEEF HASH

(1938, rewritten 1965, updated 2004)

2 lbs. freshly boiled potatoes, coarsely chopped
2 lbs. roast beef from trimmings of roasted prime ribs or top
round, coarsely chopped
1 cup beef broth
1 cup chopped, sautéed onion
salt & pepper to taste
3 Tbsp. butter
1 poached egg on each hash cake (optional)

1. Carefully mix first 4 ingredients together and season with salt & pepper. Steam in double boiler for 15 minutes.
2. For each portion, melt 1 tsp. butter in a small frying pan and place a rounded scoop of hash in it. Brown well on both sides, keeping hash cake thick and in oblong shape. (Add a little more beef broth when needed to keep hash from becoming dry.)
3. Serve on hot dinner plates with optional poached eggs, any vegetable, and a garnish of parsley.

SERVES 6

WHEN EVERYBODY ATE AT SCHRAFFT'S

14

Who Said What About Schrafft's in Over 200 Books

THE FACT THAT so many memoirs and novels mention Schrafft's speaks volumes about the stores. Whether the books heaped praise or joked about the establishments, there is no getting away from the fact that the various venues were *a presence* for many decades in the lives of countless people.

BEARD ON SCHRAFFT'S In *Epicurean Delight: Life and Times of James Beard* by Evan Jones, it's reported that Beard first discovered Schrafft's in 1924, imitating the brogues of the Irish waitresses and giving "boyish approval to the ice cream sodas snowcapped with frothy whipped cream." Another book, *James Beard's American Cookery,* credits Schrafft's with creating snacks which office workers often purchased and ate at their desks for breakfast. They were called BACON ROLLS and here's all there is to it according to Beard:

> "They are composed of soft finger rolls, similar to hot dog rolls, filled with rashers of bacon and served crisp and hot."

(Actually, in the Schrafft's recipe of 1936, rewritten in 1950, soft rolls were cut and toasted and then buttered. Two full strips of crisp, broiled bacon were then inserted in each roll.)

While there are at least 168 Schrafft's recipes for poultry, James Beard, who was aptly called "the Dean of American Cooking," plucked one of the stores' best chicken dishes for his book, *Beard on Birds.* According to Beard, "This is a recipe from the files of one of America's famous restaurant chains, Schrafft's. It makes a good dish for a dinner party or buffet."

STUFFED BREAST OF CHICKEN
WITH MUSHROOM SAUCE

4 whole chicken breasts, cut in half, boned, and poached in butter
3 cups sliced mushroom caps, sautéed (reserve the stems)
1½ Tbsp. finely chopped onion
2 Tbsp. chopped parsley
¼ cup dried bread crumbs
¼ cup heavy cream
salt & pepper
flour for dredging
finely rolled cracker crumbs
2 eggs, beaten
fresh bread crumbs
10 Tbsp. clarified butter for frying

FOR THE SAUCE
8 Tbsp. butter
½ cup flour
½ cup milk, scalded
¼ cup heavy cream
2 cups rich chicken broth
¼ cup or more Madeira

1. Cut a pocket in each cooked chicken breast. Stuff with filling made of 2 cups of the mushrooms, the onion, parsley, dried bread crumbs, heavy cream and salt & pepper to taste.

2. Flour the stuffed breasts, roll in the cracker crumbs, dip in beaten eggs, and finally roll in fresh crumbs. Quickly brown in clarified butter.

Prepare the sauce:

- Cook mushroom stems in water to cover for 10 minutes, strain, reserving liquid.
- Melt butter in saucepan and blend in flour. Cook for a minute or two, then add scalded milk, heavy cream, and chicken broth. Cook, stirring constantly, until thickened.
- Add ½ cup of reserved mushroom stem liquor, the remaining 1 cup of sauteed mushrooms, and the Madeira. Stir until blended and heated through.

SERVES 8.

James Beard was also one of the many admirers of "the precisely trimmed egg salad sandwiches" served by Schrafft's. These chopped egg and also chicken sandwiches with the crusts cut off seem to have been a lunchtime staple for many writers. Mary McCarthy nibbled them while delving into the letters of Lord Byron. E. L. Doctorow's fictional *Billy Bathgate* and his mother ordered crustless chicken sandwiches at a Schrafft's where they joined "all the fine people in the Bronx." Doctorow paints a vivid picture of that old-time, uptown Schrafft's:

> ❝I enjoyed the ceramic clatter of the restaurant, the fussy, self-important waitresses balancing their trays, the afternoon sun coming through the front window and shining on the red carpet. I liked the big-bladed silent ceiling fans turning slowly as befitting the dignity of the diners.❞

A "bread window" at the Fordham Road Schrafft's in the Bronx. E. L. Doctorow must have drawn inspiration from the place.

In *Old Books, Rare Friends: Two Literary Sleuths and Their Shared Passion,* Leona Rostenberg and her partner Madeleine B. Stern seem to have been regulars at Schrafft's on 59th Street and Madison, (same as the 58th Street store, but a different entrance). In the book, mention is made about articles being read "usually over a table at Schrafft's" and feelings expressed "over an egg salad sandwich on toasted cheese bread." Perhaps getting together at Schrafft's set the stage for those two clever women's discovery of the otherwise unknown, racy novels of another woman, Louisa May Alcott.

A character in *U.S.A.* by John Dos Passos "went to Schrafft's and had chicken patties for lunch all by herself in the middle of the crowd of cackling women shoppers." Workers and shoppers alike sandwiched Schrafft's into their plans. Or as Dorothy Sommer put it in *Generations: A Century of Women Speak About Their Lives* by Myriam Miedzian:"At that time, everything was cheap. I'd have my lunch hour at Schrafft's—beautiful, wonderful Schrafft's."

Yet another kind of Schrafft's sandwich was served up in the Pulitzer-prizewinning novel, *The Amazing Adventures of Kavalier & Clay* by Michael Gabon. While his mother lunched on stuffed peppers, the character named Tommy munched a Monte Cristo that might have been something like this . . .

WHEN EVERYBODY ATE AT SCHRAFFT'S

MONTE CRISTO TRIPLE-DECKER

3 slices of white bread
1 slice of ham
1 slice of chicken
butter for spreading
2 slices swiss cheese
3 eggs
¼ cup milk
butter for frying
jam or fruit garnish, optional

1. Butter one side of one slice of bread. Cover it with ham and chicken.
2. Butter both sides of second slice of bread. Place on top of first slice and top with cheese.
3. Butter one side of third slice of bread. Put it on top of cheese-covered slice with buttered side on top.
4. Press sandwich together. Refrigerate for a half-hour or so in foil or plastic wrap.
5. Beat eggs and milk together. Dip sandwich in mixture to coat it completely. Fry in butter , browning it on all sides.

SERVES ONE—
with a blob of jam on top or fruit slices on the side

In his autobiography, *The Ragman's Son,* Kirk Douglas writes that working at Schrafft's was pleasant, adding that "when a customer didn't finish a sandwich, you'd stuff it into your mouth as you brought it back." As to the novelist John O'Hara, it's well known that he dined more often on the contents of a bottle. In *The Art of Burning Bridges: A Life of John O'Hara*, biographer Geoffrey Wolff states that O'Hara's sister would "stand him lunch at Schrafft's when she sensed he needed nourishment. He'd recollect later in writing that he once went three days without eating."

SANDWICHES, SODAS, AND SUNDAES FONDLY REMEMBERED

THE CRUSTLESSNESS OF sandwiches seems to be as memorable to many writers as the sodas they sipped. But then Colleen Dewhurst recalls Schrafft's sodas in her autobiography and in *Notorious: The Life of Ingrid Bergman* by Donald Spoto we learn of Ingrid Bergman's penchant for the ice cream sundaes with "two scoops of vanilla" and "a double serving of hot fudge."

The composer Ned Rorem in *The Later Diaries 1961-1972* admits to having culinary dreams while overseas "not for snails in garlic, but for malteds in Schrafft's." He also wrote that "after piano rehearsals . . . during this strenuous heat wave," he would "devour quantities of Schrafft's ice cream sodas (all the color of Jennie Tourel's concert gowns during the 1940s)."

Of course, there were the legions of fans for Schrafft's hot fudge and hot butterscotch sundaes. In *Q's Legacy*, Helene

Hanff writes that Schrafft's "was the only place where I could have my martini and Gene could have her hot butterscotch sundae with toasted almonds." And in *The American Century Cookbook* by Jean Anderson, the author states that "America's very best hot fudge sauce was served at Schrafft's," confessing that when she was "younger and thinner and oblivious to calories," she went to Schrafft's on West 51st Street in Manhattan for a hot fudge sundae at least once a week. (See sauce recipes on pages 1 and 68.)

In the Madison Ave. at 58th St. store, scrumptious cakes all lined up and ready to be sold.

The baked goods also have their share of literary fame. Elia Kazan remembers an all-chocolate "shadow cake" from Schrafft's in his autobiography. In her one novel, *The Bell Jar,* Sylvia Plath has her Sylvia-like character say " . . . with my box in the plain brown paper wrapper on my lap I might have been Mrs. Anybody coming back from a day in town with a Schrafft's cake for her maiden aunt." A wedding cake on the August 1955 cover of *Bride's Magazine* was credited to

The street is clear in this photo of the West 57th St. Schrafft's, but picture it with a smashed-up wedding cake in the middle.

WHEN EVERYBODY ATE AT SCHRAFFT'S

Schrafft's. Unfortunately but humorously, in 'Tis, Frank Mc-Court writes about picking up a wedding cake at Schrafft's on West 57th Street that met with an accident. Someone dropped the box in the street and the wrecked cake had to be shoveled back into it along with the toppled bride and groom figures.

A DAILY EXPERIENCE THAT COST PRECIOUS LITTLE

IN *A Most Remarkable Fella: Frank Loesser and the Guys and Dolls in His Life by His Daughter,* Susan Loesser says that her father, who was the father of so many Broadway hits, at one time spent thirty-five cents for his meals at Schrafft's. Clifford Hood in his book, *722 Miles: The Building of the Subways and How They Transformed New York,* says the same, taking a five-cent subway ride to have "a marvelous lunch at Schrafft's for thirty-five cents," then buying a theatre ticket for fifty cents. (Loesser paid a nickel more—fifty-five cents per show.)

The novelist Judith Krantz says in *Sex and Shopping: The Confessions of a Nice Jewish Girl,* that her mother "grabbed a simple sandwich at the nearest branch of Schrafft's every single day of her working life." In *Black Sun* by Geoffrey Wolff, a character would eat lunch every day at Schrafft's with his business cronies, "where there are some pretty peppy waitresses." And the great Cole Porter made a musical rhyme out of that noonday habit: "I lunch every day at Schrafft's on chicken broth, a green salad and a Triscuit. And pistachio ice cream when I dare risk it."

BIG BUSINESS MORNING, NOON, AND NIGHT

AS REPORTED BY Harvey Levenstein in *Revolution at the Table: The Transformation of the American Diet,* "Frank G. Shattuck made a fortune out of the middle-class loss of interest in cooking by promoting his chain of Schrafft's restaurants as places where one could get the 'home cooking' which mothers no longer had the inclination to cook." In fact, apartments dwellers often left their kitchens bare, choosing to have all their meals at their neighborhood Schrafft's.

Rich folk, who wouldn't cook in any event, also wandered in for meals. Save your money for your children and go to Schrafft's where "I have luncheon every day" is the advice given in Amanda Vaill's book about the late Mark Cross millionaires, Gerald and Sara Murphy. In the sad tale *Last Wish* Betty Rollin writes, " . . . whenever my mother and I had anything weighty to discuss we'd meet at Schrafft's. There was something about the hair nets (of the Irish waitresses) and the bud vases in the center of the shiny wood tables that made us both feel safe from whatever stormy revelation one or the other of us was about to unload."

Novelists tell another story, sprinkling the stores through many of their pages. Danielle Steel takes her characters to Schrafft's in three books—*Vanished, Message from Nam,* and *The Promise* where she comes up with the memorable line about old ladies at Schrafft's stashing all their

WHEN EVERYBODY ATE AT SCHRAFFT'S

life's hopes in a shopping bag. Norine, in *The Group* by Mary McCarthy, has dinner at Schrafft's with her mother every other Wednesday. She takes home the sugar wrapped in paper marked "Schrafft's" because she says she can't get used to being rich. The Herman Wouk bestseller, *Marjorie Morningstar,* co-stars a bossy Manhattan mother type who practically lives in Schrafft's, invariably wanting to go there. "Well, it's silly to stand here in the wet," she says, "Schrafft's is just a few doors down—" And then there is the wedding party in *Raise High the Roof Beam, Carpenters* by J. D. Salinger. Suffering from the heat, they head for an air-conditioned Schrafft's to have a soda, only to find it "closed for alterations."

Schrafft's on Broadway was apparently nearby when the character, Marty, in *To Kill a Cop* by Robert Daley says he feels dressed up enough to take the girl he fancies to dinner there. "They both have the special lamb with gravy. They drink most of a bottle of sweet Portuguese rosé." The wine choice is up to you, but here is a different lamb dish from the late 1950s.

SCHRAFFT'S LAMB CHOP MIXED GRILL

(1957; 1959)

For each portion, on a hot dinner plate, place—

1 broiled loin lamb chop: on it, place—
2 slices broiled bacon (crossed over top of the chop)
1 broiled chicken liver or link sausage (on side of the chop)
1 slice grilled pineapple or 1 grilled tomato
1 helping of French fried potatoes
1 sprig of parsley for garnish

What did the beat-generation author Jack Kerouac think of Schrafft's? As you would expect, not very much. He sent a letter to his editor, Ellis Amburn, asking "what the spelling is for 'Shraffts' [*sic*] since I have no NY phonebook here to check." Having found out, he wrote the following in his novel, *Desolation Angels:* "I arrive in London in the evening . . . and go at once to a bar called 'Shakespeare.' But I might as well've walked into Schrafft's—white table cloths, quiet clinking bartenders, oak paneling . . . ugh."

To each his own!

WHEN EVERYBODY ATE AT SCHRAFFT'S

Inside, Outside, and Behind the Scenes

IN A TRADE PUBLICATION called *The Soda Fountain,* a writer reported that Schrafft's stores were "equipped with fine fixtures and decorated with dignity and taste." Not having seen the ultra-modern Schrafft's in the ESSO Building at Rockefeller Center, he observed that "In most of the stores fine selected walnut has been used for woodwork and the decorative scheme carried out in Early American period furniture." One can't help wondering what became of all that old furniture. Would anyone dare throw a chair or table away since there was surely a statement on it saying "Do not remove this tag under penalty of law."

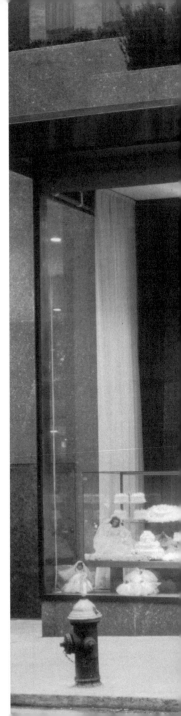

SCHRAFFT'S HITS THE BIG TIME IN ROCKEFELLER CENTER

ACCORDING TO DANIEL OKRENT in *Great Fortune—The Epic of Rockefeller Center* "After World War II . . . Schrafft's opened a restaurant that unashamedly declared itself the world's largest . . . seating 1,283 people and serving 7,500 meals a day." Customers waited, two-deep, for seats at the long counter. The flagship of Schrafft's fleet of stores, this four-level, modern extravaganza was flooded with colorful murals and sumptuous draperies. Designed by Carson and Lundin in 1947, it dominated the ESSO Building, the first building in Rockefeller Center and the tallest building in the city to be fully air conditioned.

The leather-paneled men's grill had a distinctly masculine look, or as *Architectural Forum* put it, "ridding this Schrafft's of any vestige of the Helen Hokinson feeling." Moreover, in a day-and-age of restaurants having people wash dishes by hand, the store had many, squeaky-clean kinds of mechanical equipment.

Welcome to four levels of eating and drinking in the ESSO Building, 15 West 51st Street, at Rockefeller Center.

The main dining room, a seemingly endless sea of tables.

The soda fountain & lunch counter was another long stretch of seats.

Much-needed amenities: in addition to a dishwashing machine, there were a pot washer, a glass washer, a silver washer, and even a potato peeler.

STELLAR ATTRACTION IN THE CHRYSLER BUILDING

The luxe dining room and bar in the Chrysler Building, 42nd Street at Lexington Avenue. It was part of Walter Chrysler's dream-come-true.

UNLIKE THE STREAMLINED Rockefeller Center store, the Chrysler Building Schrafft's was a study in Old World elegance. With its lavish, effervescent Rococo design by Charles E. Birge, it fit like a kidskin glove within what Walter Chrysler called his "city within a city." A first for New York and probably the nation, Chrysler's "city" contained a whole indoor community with not only its own

WHEN EVERYBODY ATE AT SCHRAFFT'S

restaurant, but also retail stores, two gymnasiums, beauty parlor, barber shop, and two emergency hospitals for men and for women. Patting himself on the back, Chrysler stated in a brochure about the skyscraper that "Every contribution to efficiency, sanitation, comfort and even inspiration, that human ingenuity can conceive or money can buy is provided." And Frank Shattuck couldn't have said it better about his dining room and bar there.

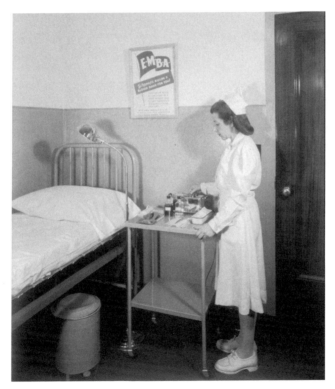

The Blood Bank Room where employees were encouraged to donate for the Red Cross.

A SHORT CLASSIC ON EAST 79TH STREET

THE LOW-RISE, WHITE marble building erected by Schrafft's on New York's East 79th Street, near Lexington Avenue, is an interesting example of the store's architectural past. Low classical columns added to its charm, but the critic Lewis Mumford felt that what he called the glamorous classical interior was cluttered up with "decorative mincings and grimacings."

According to a 79th Street resident, Burt Barnet, sundaes, sodas, and lunch food were dished out at a long mahogany counter in the front room. The serving staff

Still standing, with its classical columns intact, this former Schrafft's store now houses an antique shop.

Photograph by Lloyd H. Slomanson

working behind the counter were called "Fountain Men." Like the bartenders at other Schrafft's locations, these fellows were smartly attired. Waitresses in their ubiquitous white-aproned, black uniforms attended to the tables in the wood-paneled restaurant room. Here, dinner rules required that men wear jackets and if someone came without one, a linen jacket was provided.

SHOW-STOPPING SCHRAFFT'S ON LOWER FIFTH AVENUE

OPENED IN 1938, the store designed by Bloch & Hesse at 61 Fifth Avenue was considered by some to be a precursor to the structures in the World's Fair of 1939-1940. A showplace in its own right, this Schrafft's had a curvacious front pleasing to most eyes, but not to the critic Lewis Mumford's. While most people admired the design, Mumford called it "the new cliché," sometimes called modern, sometimes Regency, sometimes "just plain bulges."

Mumford particularly disliked "the ill-assorted windows," but had kind words to say for the interior—as well he should. With its circular, two-level design, charming murals, leather-covered chairs, and enticing food displays, the store had a sparkling personality all its own. (Today, sad to say, the building is in wretched condition and would be better off torn down.)

The interior took Schrafft's style to new heights, creating a delightful dining ambience.

The curvy façade at 61 Fifth Avenue. An odd assortment of big and little windows really lit up the place.

A SEEMINGLY ENDLESS VARIETY OF ECLECTIC STYLES

In *New York 1930,* it was stated that Charles E. Birge's designs for Schrafft's carried a message of genteel elegance to the outer boroughs. For example, the restaurant at 912 Flatbush Avenue, Brooklyn, opposite Erasmus Hall High School, was a major social focus of a historic neighborhood. Back in Manhattan, the stores mixed and matched different design elements. A case in point: the 383 Fifth Avenue Schrafft's was described as having a richly appointed interior in the front with a Colonial-style tearoom at the rear. And the Schrafft's store at 20 West Thirty-eighth Street had a Georgian look, while its mezzanine tearoom was Italian.

At 383 Fifth Avenue, Schrafft's was a neighbor to the most popular department stores, the perfect spot to attract and feed the ladies who shopped.

According to the book, the large Schrafft's at 13 East Forty-second Street, which opened in 1923, "combined an ornate double-height polychromed Italianate candy shop with a much more spare Colonial-style mezzanine dining gallery, which had wood paneling and Ionic pilasters painted soft green and a Georgian-style men's grill on the third floor finished

in American walnut." The authors added that the façades of this and many other Schrafft's establishments combined black and gold marble pilasters, bronze-trimmed windows, and bronze signage."

The multi-storied Schrafft's at 18 East 42nd Street had different decorating styles on each floor.

It is a crying shame that we no longer have all those popular dining places. Where did they go and why? Andy Warhol said his favorite restaurant atmosphere had always been that of the good, plain, American lunchroom. The old-style Schrafft's and the old-style Chock Full O' Nuts were absolutely the only things in the world that he was truly nostalgic for. He had one possible explanation for the Schrafft's stores' departure:

> "Schrafft's restaurants were the beauties of their day, and then they tried to keep up with the times and they modified and modified until they lost all their charm and were bought by a big company. But if they could just have kept their same look and style, and held on through the lean years when they weren't in style, today they'd be the best thing around. You have to hang on in periods when your style isn't popular, because if it's good, it'll come back, and you'll be a recognized beauty once again."
>
> —*The Philosophy of Andy Warhol*

As to how Schrafft's could disappear from the scene, keep in mind that the stores lasted *for over seven decades.* Today, according to the New York State Restaurant Association, "almost seventy percent of New York's 23,000 food establishments close or change hands within their first five years."

The first "big company" Warhol may have been referring to was the St. Louis-based Pet Inc. In 1968, when Schrafft's was a fifty-five-restaurant chain with outlets in eight or more states, they merged with Pet and with Pet's backing they took aim at a wider audience. The wild Warhol sixty-second commercial for Schrafft's, described on page 71, is an example of the attempted change of image. Another TV commercial at the time showed sexy-looking young women in miniskirts with the line, "Have you seen the little old ladies in Schrafft's lately?" Some of the New York City stores even went in for a little remodeling to make their bar areas as conspicuous as their soda fountains.

Ten years later, The Riese Organization came on the scene. Their powerful restaurant operation acquired 26 Schrafft's stores in 1978, and ate deeply into the New York City market through the acquisition of many chains. In the Riese corporate history, it's explained that they purchased well-located restaurants like Schrafft's that had below-market, long-term leases. And what was considered prime real estate in 1978, the organization states, is even more prime today.

But let's backtrack . . .

16

A New York Institution: The Schrafft's Walk Guides

THIS PROMOTIONAL EFFORT was of great service to the city *and* to Schrafft's. In these booklets, street-by-street maps pointed out places to see and savor while of course pinpointing the Schrafft's locations in each neighborhood. The nine walking tours took city dwellers as well as tourists from areas listed as Wall Street, Downtown, Empire State, Forty-second Street, Rockefeller Center, Midtown/East Side, Upper Midtown, Upper Midtown/West Side, and Uptown/East Side.

A HUGELY successful project, the Walk Guides went to many editions. Hundreds of thousands of copies were published after the first edition came out in 1964 for World's Fair visitors. (The author had kept a copy through the years.) Many of the suggested sites are still in existence and worth seeing even though you can no longer stop off at a Schrafft's store along the way.

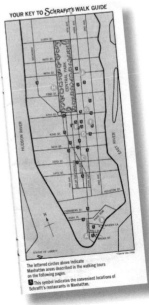

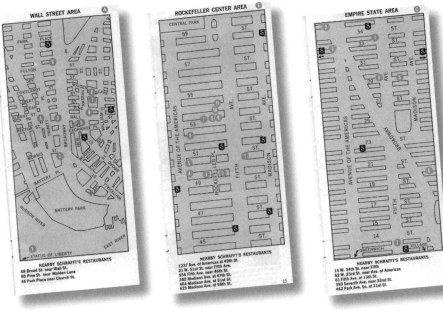

WALL STREET AREA — A

NEARBY SCHRAFFT'S RESTAURANTS
48 Broad St. near Wall St.
80 Pine St. near Maiden Lane
46 Park Place near Church St.

ROCKEFELLER CENTER AREA — E

NEARBY SCHRAFFT'S RESTAURANTS
1237 Ave. of Americas near 49th St.
21 W. 51st St. near Fifth Ave.
556 Fifth Ave. near 46th St.
382 Madison Ave. at 51st St.
464 Madison Ave. at 58th St.
625 Madison Ave. at 58th St.

13

EMPIRE STATE AREA — C

NEARBY SCHRAFFT'S RESTAURANTS
15 W. 34th St. near Fifth
62 W. 23rd St. near Ave. of Americas
61 Fifth Ave. at 13th St.
393 Seventh Ave. near 32nd St.
462 Park Ave. So. at 31st St.

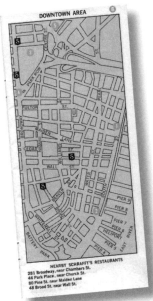

DOWNTOWN AREA — B

NEARBY SCHRAFFT'S RESTAURANTS
281 Broadway, near Chambers St.
46 Park Place, near Church St.
80 Pine St. near Maiden Lane
48 Broad St. near Wall St.

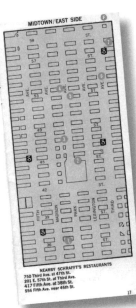

MIDTOWN/EAST SIDE — F

NEARBY SCHRAFFT'S RESTAURANTS
750 Third Ave. at 47th St.
201 E. 57th St. at Third Ave.
417 Fifth Ave. at 38th St.
556 Fifth Ave. near 46th St.

17

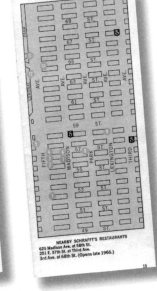

UPPER MIDTOWN AREA — G

NEARBY SCHRAFFT'S RESTAURANTS
625 Madison Ave. at 58th St.
201 E. 57th St. at Third Ave.
3rd Ave. at 68th St. (Opens late 1966.)

19

A SCHRAFFT'S WHEREVER YOU WENT—
ON-THE-TOWN OR OUT-OF-TOWN

IN ADDITION TO the many Manhattan locations in the Walk Guides, listings are included in the back for Schrafft's stores in the Bronx, Brooklyn, Westchester County, Newark, NJ, and five in the greater Boston, MA area. What's more—are you ready?—there were the Schrafft's restaurants, restaurants and motor inns, and restaurants with adjoining approved motor inns, at one time or another, in Syracuse, NY, Buffalo, NY, Albany, NY, Rochester, NY, Binghamton, NY, and Niagara Falls, NY. Laurel and Baltimore, MD were on the list, as were Providence, RI, Cleveland, Ohio, and Troy, Michigan. In Pennsylvania: Jenkintown, Reading, Harrisburg, Pittsburgh, Monroeville, and two in downtown Philadelphia. In Connecticut: New London and Waterbury. Down south, Schrafft's could be sighted in High Point, NC, Atlanta, GA, and Richmond, VA, along with Floridian outposts in Boca Raton, Palm Beach, Clearwater, St. Petersburg Beach, Bal Harbour, and Ft. Lauderdale. Even California got into the act with a Schrafft's in Beverly Hills and two others in Los Angeles.

A highly unusual Schrafft's was in the Monroeville Mall Ice Palace near Pittsburgh, PA. Opened in 1969, the mall had the first full-size ice arena in an East Coast shopping center, starring a skating rink larger than the one at Rockefeller Plaza. Schrafft's was the mall's only fine-dining restaurant. Appropriately enough, it featured an ice skating

decor. And for live entertainment, all those skaters gliding along or slipping and sliding could be viewed from the windows of the rink-side, terraced dining room.

Just minutes from downtown Rochester, NY, this very modern Schrafft's Restaurant/Motor Inn thrived until it was destroyed in a 1978 fire.

TAKE ME OUT . . .

AS ANY OLD sports fan knows, America's interest in base-ball goes way back, but the real glory days in areas dotted with Schrafft's stores were when the New York Yankees slugged it out against the Brooklyn Dodgers during the World Series. Imagine seeing brilliant Bronx bombers like Mickey Mantle and Yogi Berra battling against such great Dodgers as Pee Wee Reese and Jackie Robinson. Then picture the Dodger lovers at Ebbets Field going stark raving mad when their team finally won the Series in 1955. The Yanks took the honors from them in 1941, 1947, 1949, 1952, 1953, and again in 1956. Yet needless to say, the stadiums were packed on all those "subway series" days—and one can assume, so were all the Schrafft's in whichever of the two boroughs, the Bronx or Brooklyn, the games were being played. Peanuts and popcorn and Cracker Jacks may have been fine from inning to inning, but afterwards it must have been nice to be able to celebrate or commiserate with real drinks and food.

And let's not forget the never-ending war between the Yankees and the Red Sox. Just as crowds flocked to the Bronx, they also sped to Boston to watch the two teams lock horns. The rivalry dates back to 1901 and fortunately for the fans, Boston was home base for Schrafft's as well as the Red Sox.

"The daintiest last, to make the end most sweet."

— WILLIAM SHAKESPEARE

I**T TOOK A** strong woman or man to walk out of a Schrafft's store without purchasing some of the sweet treats to take home or back to the office. Like the seductive powers of a siren, they beckoned to you in window displays before you even went inside. They seemed to be whispering "Life is uncertain. Eat dessert first."

Heartfelt chocolate gifts for Valentine's Day at 58th Street. and Madison Avenue. And dozens of different alluring baked goods in a front window at 1381 Broadway.

A COUNTER ATTACK ON ANYONE'S DIET

THE CALORIFIC "C" words—Candy, Cookies and Cakes—were always in abundance.

At one time, the New York School of Ballet was right above a Schrafft's, a fact that led one balletomane to wonder how those skinny dancers could keep to their diets with all those confections in sight.

In *O, The Oprah Magazine,* Patricia Volk wrote that she practically grew up in her neighborhood Schrafft's when and where a square of the dark fudge she loved cost seven cents. If that sounds cheap, consider that sizable chocolate bars once cost only a nickel and there was also such a thing as "penny candy—candy for a penny." But the biggest bargain may have been Schrafft's boxed chocolates . . . 60¢ per pound? $1 per pound? Have you checked out the price of a good box of chocolates nowadays?

You could have the chocolates for a song in more ways than one. In the 1930s, some of the advertising took the form of 78 rpm records called SCHRAFFT'S PLAY-A-TUNE. Records "for every occasion" serenaded listeners with sweet music, presumably while they nibbled the stores' sweet chocolates.

Author of the witty, nostalgic book, *Stuffed: Adventures of a Restaurant Family* (not the Shattucks), Volk said in an interview that the food she misses the most is Schrafft's fudge. She rhapsodized on what made it so good: "It's an extremely complex taste. I think they put brandy or cognac in it. It lingers and it's sweet, but it has a sultry undertone. It had the perfect texture too. It was the best ever, and they've discontinued it. I've heard that Julia Child was also a Schrafft's fudge lover. I was going to write and invite her to spend an afternoon together to see if we could come up with the recipe."

Although the following hand-scrawled fudge recipe contains no brandy or cognac, it could be what Patricia Volk was looking for. Found in a Shattuck family note-book, it must have been used in Schrafft's. However, it is incomplete and slightly difficult to decipher. But per-haps an enthusiast like Ms. Volk could fill in the blanks and piece it together.

> Choc Fudge ✓
> 4 cups sugar   — 1 tsp salt —
> 1 cup milk   — 3 sq. choc —
> cook together till boils about
> 10 min — should make
> string 3" to 4" long —
> then add butter & vanilla

As to the idea of Schrafft's lacing anything with spirits, it's highly possible. Witness these family recipes used in or derived from ones at Schrafft's.

MOTHER'S WHISKEY SAUCE

—For a Christmas pudding

1. Bring ½ cup sugar and ¼ cup water to a boil. Slowly add l well-beaten egg.
2. Cook and stir until it thickens. Add whiskey to suit your taste.

SCHRAFFT'S BRANDY SAUCE

—For pudding or cake

¼ cup flour
1 Tbsp. fresh lemon juice
2 cups butter
1¾ cups sugar
¼ cup boiling water
6 Tbsp. Brandy

1. Melt butter in heavy pan. Add sugar and flour that have been well combined.

2. Mix in lemon juice and pour in boiling water. Boil
   again for 3 minutes, then add the Brandy. Yield: 10
   portions

MEMORABLE, MUCH LOVED COOKIES
(AND SOME OLD ONES THAT MAY BE NEW TO YOU)

AMONG THE ITEMS that Schrafft's regulars still long for
are the cookies. They lured customers on the way out of
the stores and were often devoured before reaching home.
The Butterscotch Cookies and Chewy Oatmeal Cookies
are so delectable, recipes for them can now be found on
the internet and in some cookbooks. But we have that
great food writer and food historian JUDITH JONES to
thank for adapting them for home kitchens and writing
recipe instructions. Judith acquired the original formu-
las from the Schrafft's kitchen thanks, she says, to James
Beard. But she took on the task of cutting down the huge
amounts and making up for the industrial ingredients used
by Schrafft's. Judith adds, "Schraffts was so much a part of
my childhood—always the place we went to after school
for a soda and a shake. And of course, their cookies were
heavenly."

SCHRAFFT'S BUTTERSCOTCH COOKIES

2 Tbsp. butter at room temperature
¾ cup vegetable shortening, such as Crisco,
at room temperature
1¼ cups dark brown sugar
1 egg
2 Tbsp. nonfat dry milk
1 Tbsp. vanilla
1¾ cups flour
½ tsp. baking soda
½ tsp. salt
1 cup finely chopped pecans

1. Preheat the oven to 375°. Grease baking sheets.
2. Combine the butter and shortening in a bowl and beat for a few seconds. Add the sugar and beat until creamy. Add the egg, dry milk, and vanilla and beat until light.
3. Combine the flour, baking soda, and salt in a bowl. Stir with a fork to mix and lighten. Add to the butter mixture and blend well. Stir in pecans and mix well.
4. Drop heaping tablespoons of dough 2 inches apart onto the baking sheet.
5. Dip the bottom of a 3-inch diameter drinking glass into flour and use it to press the dough into

a circle of the same dimension. If the dough sticks a little as you lift off the glass, scrape it from the glass. Pat any bits back into the circle of dough to make it even and neatly round. Dip the glass into flour after each use.

6. Bake the cookies for 7 to 10 minutes, or until golden brown. Remove from the oven and gently lift the cookies onto a cooling rack. Let cool completely, then store in an airtight container. Yield: about 30 cookies

SCHRAFFT'S OF BOSTON CHEWY OATMEAL COOKIES

As scrumptious as the cookies were in New York City, it's been said that this Boston version was considered to be even better. In fact, real cookie lovers would actually go out of their way, taking the train to Boston to buy them. Here's the recipe with no travel time required.

1½ cups old-fashioned or quick-cooking rolled oats (not instant oatmeal)
1¼ cups all-purpose flour
½ tsp. baking powder
½ tsp. baking soda
½ tsp. salt

1 tsp. ground cinnamon
½ tsp. ground allspice
¼ lb (1 stick) unsalted butter, softened
¾ cup sugar
¼ cup packed dark brown sugar
2 eggs
1 tsp. vanilla extract
¼ cup whole or lowfat milk
1 cup raisins
1 cup chopped walnuts

1. Preheat oven to 350°. Lightly grease 2 cookie sheets.
2. Whisk together the rolled oats, flour, baking powder, baking soda, salt, cinnamon, and allspice in a large bowl.
3. Using an electric mixer, cream the butter with the two sugars in a large bowl until smooth. Add the eggs and vanilla and beat until light and well blended. With the mixer on low speed, add the oat mixture and the milk, beating until well combined and a stiff dough forms. Stir in the raisins and nuts. (If not using immediately, refrigerate the dough for up to 12 hours.) Drop the dough by tablespoonfuls onto the cookie sheets, spacing about 2 inches apart. Press the tops gently to flatten very slightly.
4. Bake until the edges are brown and the centers are still soft and puffy, about 11 to 14 minutes. Cool

on wire racks. Store in a covered container for up to 3 days or freeze. Yield: about 3 dozen cookies.

OTHER CRUNCHY COOKIE INDULGENCES

LESS WELL-KNOWN today are the cookies that started out in the wood stoves of the Schraffts and Shattucks. Reminiscing, one family member waxed poetic about the sight, smell, and flavor of the cookies that were created in the old kitchens on autumn afternoons around 1942. Baked on large, buttered cookie sheets so that their sugary bottoms carmelized, the cookies were placed on a table to cool and then layered between sheets of wax paper. It didn't matter if you weren't at all hungry, the fresh-from-the-oven aroma would awaken your appetite.

Frank Shattuck, the great-grandson of the first Frank Shattuck, says he gets hungry just thinking of the molasses cookies and the sour cream cookies his grandmother baked for the family—recipes over 75 years old that made their way into cookies that became popular in the Schrafft's stores. One version offered here became a commercial success in Aunt Kittie and Aunt Jennie Shattuck's "Buy a Cake Shop" which was the forerunner of Schrafft's stores. At home, such molasses cookies were often served with extra-soft butter spread on top, accompanied by a glass of whole milk rich with cream.

OLD-FASHIONED MOLASSES COOKIES

1 cup butter at room temperature
1 cup Crisco at room temperature★
1 cup sugar
6 eggs, beaten
2 cups molasses
1 cup raisins
1 cup hot water
2 tsp. baking soda
2 tsp. cinnamon
7 cups flour
★*Original recipe specifies ½ cup Crisco, ½ cup chicken fat.*

1. Preheat oven to 325°. Blend butter, Crisco and sugar together. Mix in eggs, molasses, raisins, and water. Sift soda, cinnamon and flour into the batter.
2. Drop batter from tablespoons onto large, buttered cookie sheets. Bake 10 to 12 minutes until brown. "Makes 8 dozen," according to Aunt Kittie.

In addition to slews of Molasses Cookie recipes— obviously a popular choice—there were also some appealing Sour Cream Sugar Cookies, made with or without lard. While lard was once a baked goods staple, it fell out of favor. So even "Mother" often switched to cookies without it.

MOTHER'S SOUR CREAM
SUGAR COOKIES

2 eggs
2 cups sugar
1 cup sour cream
¾ cup butter
1 tsp. lemon juice
1 tsp. baking soda
1 tsp. baking powder
2 tsp. nutmeg
4 cups flour

1. Preheat oven to 350°.
2. Beat together, eggs, sugar, sour cream, butter, and lemon juice.
3. Sift into batter, baking soda, baking powder, nutmeg, and flour.
4. Grease pans and drop batter from dessert spoon. Sprinkle with sugar and press a big raisin or two in centers. Bake until brown, 10-12 minutes.

WHEN EVERYBODY ATE AT SCHRAFFT'S

CANDY IS DANDY, AND HOW ABOUT THOSE BAKED GOODS!

SCHRAFFT'S HAD CANDY factories not only in Boston, but also in Brooklyn, where their famous Wafer Thin Mints were made. Try as they did, other companies were unable to produce the uniquely square and incredibly thin product. On an old TV whodunit, the detective constantly carried an unmistakable box of the mints, periodically offering them to all comers. And in Alex Cherry's book, *Yankee, R.N.*, about an American in the Royal Navy, the author tells about stocking Schrafft's mints among the delicacies to take to friends in England. Cherry told a member of the Shattuck family that the Wafer Thin Mints were prized not only for their taste, but because they were an excellent preventive for seasickness.

Also incomparable, the baked goods were produced in their own New York factory attached to the executive offices on West 23rd Street. There, *all those beloved bakery recipes seem to have disappeared!* More's the pity, because the breads, cakes, and pies were sooo delectable. In fact, the apple pie was such a treasure, it won hands down in a citywide restaurant contest. Frank G. Shattuck would have liked that. What could be more American?

However, here is one piece of advice if you want to try and bake a Schrafft's-quality apple pie. *Use only Northern Spy apples.* They were the secret ingredient.

THANKS FOR THE MEMORY!

AFTER TASTING A mere morsel of the little cake called a petite madeleine, Marcel Proust's vast *Remembrance of Things Past* came alive. Today, just the mention of the desserts and other food at the old Schrafft's establishments brings back a flood of personal memories. Here are just a few . . .

> *I was in the U.S. Navy during WWII. I missed Schrafft's hot fudge sundaes so much, I was determined to duplicate them aboard ship. Going through the Panama Canal when I had plenty of time off, I experimented in the galley and, modesty aside, made a sauce almost as good as Schrafft's.*
> —*Mike Cantor*

> *My old beau and I had a regular Saturday routine. Before going to a matinee at the movies, we would have delicious chicken salad sandwiches at our favorite Schrafft's and after the show, we would stop by to buy a pint of ice cream to enjoy later.*
> —*Lee Klang*

> *What I remember most fondly about Schrafft's was that I could go there and have a cocktail, all by myself, and nobody cared or stared.*
> —*Barbara Malley*

Whenever my grandparents were in the neighborhood, they would take me to the New York Schrafft's at Broadway and 82nd Street. They liked it because it reminded them of their favorite Boston tearooms.

—*Aaron Frankel*

Schrafft's was the class place to be, especially among those of us who wore white kidskin gloves.

—*Libby Evans*

My wife and I moved from New York at the end of the fifties. Every time we return for a visit, we take a bus ride down memory lane, looking around for changes. Spotting where any Schrafft's used to be, we reminisce about the sundaes and chicken à la king and no-crust egg salad sandwiches.

—*Jack Rothman*

My very Irish great-uncle brought me to the Bronx to meet his sister who was in a convent. We took an elevated train, walked down the stairs, and Schrafft's was there. He liked Schrafft's because it was of the Irish persuasion, but he always told me to order the Yankee Pot Roast.

—*Kathy Campo*

Here's proof that the Schrafft's era was "the age of innocence." My friends and I left our babies outside in their carriages while we went inside to sip Schrafft's sodas.

—*Molly Moed*

"THE DAINTIEST LAST..."

When I was a little girl my English grandmother visited from London and took me to Schrafft's. When her tea was served, she became enraged because she thought there was a mouse in it. Coming from a country where tea was always brewed, she didn't recognize a teabag.

—*Susan Locke Rubens*

Growing up in Brooklyn, I used to be called Miss Schrafft's by my father because I loved going there and eating the ice cream so much.

—*Sydelle Ross*

When I was a young attorney, I frequented Schrafft's all over Manhattan—especially the stylish one on Fifth Avenue at 13th Street and the five-story Schrafft's on Fifth Avenue at 46th Street. In particular, I loved their curried shrimp and chicken pot pie.

—*Richard Estes*

In the days when I did some modeling, a friend and I regularly lunched at Schrafft's. She is part Japanese, part Hungarian, and a great cook. On her recommendation, we dined on Chicken Chow Mein★ of all things! It was very good.

—*Patricia Theilheimer*

★Author's note: The Chow Mein and what Schrafft's called Oriental Chicken were pure Americana.

Epilogue

THIS STATEMENT TO employees in a Schrafft's newsletter goes a long way to explain how the restaurants survived and thrived for so many decades . . .

"It is the way we do our jobs, both behind the scenes and in meeting the customers, that establishes the public opinion of our Company. The sparkling china and glass, the careful following of a recipe, the friendly, pleasant selling manner and service, all add up to a good impression of Schrafft's.

For Mr. and Mrs. Customer, we are as much Schrafft's as our products. Let us accept the challenge in those words and see that Schrafft's reputation for quality merchandise is matched with a reputation for quality people."

Recipe Index

Index of Names

INDEX OF NAMES

About the author

JOAN KANEL SLOMANSON is the author of *A Short History: Thumbnail Sketches of 50 Little Giants* along with several books of humor. A history buff and an accomplished cook, her interest in the culinary arts was sparked by the College of Human Ecology at Cornell University of which she is a graduate and led to advertising and promotional writing on many food and beverage accounts.

Of special note here: For several years, Slomanson helped to create and promote various restaurants.

A former advertising agency creative director, Slomanson has also written fund-raising

Photograph by Eric Slomanson

pieces and speeches to benefit the HRH Princess Elizabeth of Yugoslavia Foundation. Her other public service work included a ten-year term on the board of directors of Empire Blue Cross and Blue Shield where she chaired the health maintenance organization committee. She also served as a director and corporate secretary on the boards of Managed Health, Inc. and CHP-The Medical Group.

A resident of New York City, she is married to the architect and photographer Lloyd ("Woody") Slomanson. They have two sons named Peter and Eric, two cats named Franny and Zooey, and a bird called Dovey.